Nobody's Fool

A comedy

Simon Williams

Samuel French — London
www.samuelfrench-london.co.uk

Copyright © 2006 by Simon Williams
All Rights Reserved

NOBODY'S FOOL is fully protected under the copyright laws of the British Commonwealth, including Canada, the United States of America, and all other countries of the Copyright Union. All rights, including professional and amateur stage productions, recitation, lecturing, public reading, motion picture, radio broadcasting, television and the rights of translation into foreign languages are strictly reserved.

ISBN 978-0-573-11518-9
www.samuelfrench.co.uk
www.samuelfrench.com

FOR AMATEUR PRODUCTION ENQUIRIES

**UNITED KINGDOM AND WORLD
EXCLUDING NORTH AMERICA**
plays@samuelfrench.co.uk
020 7255 4302/01

Each title is subject to availability from Samuel French, depending upon country of performance.

CAUTION: Professional and amateur producers are hereby warned that NOBODY'S FOOL is subject to a licensing fee. Publication of this play does not imply availability for performance. Both amateurs and professionals considering a production are strongly advised to apply to the appropriate agent before starting rehearsals, advertising, or booking a theatre. A licensing fee must be paid whether the title is presented for charity or gain and whether or not admission is charged.

The Professional Rights in this play are controlled by Peters, Fraser and Dunlop, Drury House, 34-43 Russell Street, London WC2B 5HA.

No one shall make any changes in this title for the purpose of production. No part of this book may be reproduced, stored in a retrieval system, or transmitted in any form, by any means, now known or yet to be invented, including mechanical, electronic, photocopying, recording, videotaping, or otherwise, without the prior written permission of the publisher. No one shall upload this title, or part of this title, to any social media websites.

The right of Simon Williams to be identified as author of this work has been asserted in accordance with Section 77 of the Copyright, Designs and Patents Act 1988.

NOBODY'S FOOL

First presented as **BOYS WILL BE BOYS** at the Mill at Sonning Dinner Theatre on 24th June 2003 with the following cast:

Lenny	Simon Williams
Gus	Gareth Thomas
Dee Dee	Amy Williams
Fran	Karen Ascoe
Letitia	Sheila Ballantine

Directed by Simon Williams
Set designed by Jaqueline Hutson

Subsequently presented as **NOBODY'S FOOL** by Ian Fricker for Nobody's Fool Ltd at the Devonshire Park Theatre, Eastbourne, on 28th September 2004, with the following cast:

Lenny	Simon Williams
Gus	Bernard Kay
Dee Dee	Chloe Newsome
Fran	Louise Jameson
Letitia	Joanna Van Gyseghem

Directed by Andy de la Tour
Designed by Julie Godfrey

CHARACTERS

Lenny, a statistician, middle-aged
Gus, Lenny's father, 60s
Dee Dee, Lenny's daughter, late teens
Fran, Lenny's ex-wife, middle-aged
Letitia Butters, a TV presenter, of a certain age

The action of the play takes place in the living-room and basement study of Lenny's house in Twickenham

Time — the present

Other plays by Simon Williams published by Samuel French

Kiss of Death
Laying the Ghost
Nobody's Perfect

ACT I

The living-room and basement study of a large old house in Twickenham. The present. Early autumn

The living-room is R, the basement study L, the idea being that in fact the living-room is directly above the study. There are two exits from the living-room, one the front door of the house, the other an archway giving access to a landing from which lead the stairs to the basement. The living-room is furnished with a sofa, chair and cupboard and a desk on which there are a laptop computer and an intercom. There is a small video camera on a tripod DS, *with a microphone; a bottle of wine and some glasses stand on a shelf. Three exits lead from the study: a spiral staircase leading to the landing, a door to a kitchen and a front door on to the basement area. An integral fish tank has been set into the wall. The room is furnished with a chair or two and a desk with a laptop, an intercom, a normal telephone and a framed photograph on it. A chart lies on a shelf and there is a broom handle by the desk*

The CURTAIN *rises. Both rooms are lit. Lenny is sitting at the study desk, typing*

Lenny (*reading as he types*) "Joshua gazed at Ingrid. The storm was raging outside as they took refuge in the cave far above Lake Windermere. There were pearls of rain in her hair and her eyes were shining in the half light. The silence between them was like a — was like a — was enormous." (*He picks up a photograph*) "As he gazed at her, he thought to himself — 'Did you ever really love me?' (*Typing and reading again*) "As he gazed at her he cleared his throat and said —— "

Lenny types through the following

Gus enters the living-room singing a rock song, happily and indistinctly. He adjusts the camera, dancing a bit. He plugs in a lead from the camera to the laptop. He is very pleased to see himself on screen and blows a corny kiss at himself

Gus And cue Gus. Action.

Gus exits to prepare himself

Lenny (*reading as he types*) "And said — 'That is quite a storm.' Ingrid nodded, 'All this climate change', Joshua said, 'it's caused by the holes in the ozone layer.'"

Gus enters the living-room in a black hat and dark glasses. He has a stick-on moustache and a fat cigar and carries some cue cards

Gus (*to the camera, very casually*) Hi there. Welcome to the London home of the country's favourite writer of romantic fiction, Myrtle Banbury — wait for the applause ... (*He checks his notes*) Oh, I see — yes, yes of course — wait for the applause. Myrtle Banbury — clap clap clap. Last year Myrtle won the Purple Kiss award and her new novel — (*he checks his notes*) *Boys Will Be Boys* is due out this Christmas.

The telephone rings. Gus answers it

(*Into the telephone*) Hallo. Gus Loftus. ... Hi there, Felicity. ... You want to talk to Myrtle about the book? I'm afraid Myrtle is in — (*he checks his notes*) South America. ... But her mobile is only for emergencies. ... Sure. ... What? ... Ciao to you too. (*He stamps on the floor*)

In the study, Lenny looks up at his ceiling, then pokes it with the broom handle

In the living-room Gus answers with a stamp

Lenny reluctantly presses a button on the intercom. (NB: The conversations on the intercom are not actually amplified but we have the impression they are)

Lenny (*into the intercom*) Hi, Dad. I thought you'd gone away.
Gus (*into the intercom*) I'm back. Your publisher is on the warpath. She's going to ring you.
Lenny (*into the intercom*) Me? Me, Lenny Loftus, the boring statistician?
Gus (*into the intercom*) Is it likely?
Lenny (*into the intercom*) You mean me, Myrtle Banbury, queen of chick lit? On the pink phone? What does she want?
Gus Perhaps you've got to take a medical. Could be fun.

In the study, a mobile telephone rings with a special tone

Lenny Oh bloody hell. (*Into the intercom*) Thanks. Bye.

Gus exits

Lenny produces a mobile phone — the "Myrtle" mobile — clears his throat, does a quick scale and answers as "Myrtle"

Act I

(Into the pink telephone) Hallo. ... Myrtle Banbury here. ... Oh Felicity, what a surprise. ... Hm? ... Yes, I'm in India. ... Did he? ... Silly me, of course I'm in South America. ... How can I help? ... The last chapter? Oh, it's coming along. ... The trouble is Joshua is a great big wuss, is he? ... He needs to pull his finger out. ... Right. ... *Ciao* to you too. (*He hangs up. To himself*) Pull his finger out? Some fat chance. (*He puts the pink phone in a drawer and resumes his work*)

Gus enters the living-room

Gus (*trying a different tone and style*) Yes, this is where Myrtle stays during her rare visits to these shores. How do I know? Because I'm her personal manager Gus Loftus, the mover and shaker behind the enigma we all know as Myrtle Banbury.

Lenny activates the intercom. The following conversation takes place entirely over the intercom

Lenny So you're back already. I thought you were away at a seventies festival in Haywards Heath.
Gus I was.
Lenny With the Dolly Parton look-alike.
Gus Brenda from the *Dog and Duck*. Her car broke down. How are things down there?
Lenny You are talking to a very tired grumpy old woman.
Gus Myrtle got writer's block, has she?
Lenny She's utterly constipated. By the way, what's a wuss?
Gus A wuss? Is something between a pillock and a twat.
Lenny Thanks. Is Dee Dee home yet?
Gus No.
Lenny I heard voices.
Gus I was rehearsing.
Lenny Rehearsing what?
Gus Have you forgotten? We are doing "Mind Your Own Business": "The Letitia Butters Show."
Lenny I beg your pardon?
Gus It's a top-rated show, Lenny. Especially the fly-on-the-wall section.
Lenny Fly-on-the-wall? Here?
Gus Yup ... It'll be fantastic for the book launch. The sales will be humongous. I did tell you about it.
Lenny You said had I ever seen the show?
Gus And you said yes.
Lenny Yes, I said yes, I'd seen it. Not, yes, I'd do it. I'm absolutely not doing it, Dad.

Gus It's too late, Lenny — it starts tomorrow. They'll be doing the rig.
Lenny The rig?
Gus The hidden camera and stuff.
Lenny Camera?
Gus For the fly-on-the-wall section of the show. The video diary. And then in comes Letitia and — kapow! (*As Letitia*) "This is Letitia Butters telling you to 'Mind Your Own Business'."

Dee Dee enters the living-room

Gus puts a finger up to his lips

Lenny This is not going to happen, Dad, do you hear? No cameras, no flies on no walls, no rig, no kapow, none of it, OK?
Gus (*grimacing at the intercom*) OK.
Lenny And don't make faces, Dad, the wind might change — not that anybody would notice.
Gus Thank you. Get back to work and I'll bring you down some syrup of figs.

Gus takes his finger off the intercom. Dee Dee hugs Gus

Lenny exits to the kitchen

Dee Dee (*studying Gus' outfit*) Hi, Grampi — joined the Mafia, have you? (*She pulls off his moustache*)
Gus Ow. I was practising for Letitia tomorrow. I want to be a sports presenter.
Dee Dee What happened to Haywards Heath — the Dolly Parton look-alike?
Gus Her car broke down. She had a puncture.
Dee Dee Don't tell me.
Gus Near side front.
Dee Dee (*groaning and holding her hand out*) That'll be one pound.
Gus (*giving Dee Dee a pound*) A pound? Why not fifty p?
Dee Dee It's fifty p for a bad pun, Grampi. It's a pound for a sexual innuendo.
Gus Innuendo? Would that be an Italian suppository? (*He pays some more*) Your dad's gone a bit wobbly about "Mind Your Own Business".
Dee Dee Leave him to me. Letitia can be pretty daunting.
Gus I think she's quite sexy.
Dee Dee Letitia? You are so rancid.
Gus The way to handle women like that is to treat them like babes, flirt with them.
Dee Dee No, no, no, Grampi. Don't do the flirting thing with Letitia Butters. It's unspeakable when you do that. I saw you with that aromatherapist at The Neighbourhood Watch Disco — all that business with your nostrils flared and your head sort of waggling about. (*She demonstrates*) "Yo. Would you like one of my smoky bacon crisps, honey child?"

Act I

Gus That's called suave, Dee Dee. She said I'd got something of Clint Eastwood about me.
Dee Dee "The Good, The Bad and The Grampi". Why can't you be your age?
Gus I don't like my age. I hate being fifty-nine.
Dee Dee Sixty-seven.
Gus Sixty-one.
Dee Dee Sixty-three.
Gus Sold. Inside the body of this decrepit dirty old man there's a decrepit dirty young one trying to get out.
Dee Dee Keep him in, Grampi, keep him in. Letitia Butters is a very cool powerful woman. Plus, she's a medium, remember.
Gus Well, they can't all be D-cups.
Dee Dee (*with her hand out*) That'll be another pound. She is a very spiritual woman, Grampi. She's always going on about auras; she gets vibrations.
Gus (*handing over the money*) That's what comes of sitting on the spin dryer. Load of old cobblers.
Dee Dee Just you be very careful with her, Grampi. What does Dad need syrup of figs for anyway?
Gus He needs to loosen up. Myrtle's got a bit of a blockage. I'm going to rehearse — see what you think. (*He puts his moustache, hat and glasses back on*)
Dee Dee Keep it cool, Grampi, loosey goosey ... .
Gus Loosey goosey — right.

Lenny enters the living-room and sees the following rehearsal

(*Performing with his cigar*) Hi, there, folks ... Welcome to Myrtle Banbury's London pad. She's one cool chick is Myrtle, I can tell you.
Lenny Stop it. Stop it. This is not happening.
Dee Dee Hi, Dad.
Lenny Hallo, my darling. (*Looking at Gus*) Dad, what is this, a *Godfather* convention? What is going on?
Gus I want to break into television.
Lenny They'll shoot you. What is that thing on your upper lip?
Gus It's a moustache, clever clogs; it's called a Banderos.
Lenny Have you got it on upside down?
Gus That's the trouble with you, my boy — no vision.
Lenny You look like a cross between Saddam Hussein and Fungus the Bogeyman.
Gus I need a suave veneer.
Lenny (*dismantling the camera and stowing it*) You need embalming fluid.
Dee Dee The new book has to be promoted, Dad.
Lenny No.
Dee Dee The filming will only take a couple of days — it's a breeze.

Lenny No.
Dee Dee Just a few snippets of video diary and a short interview with Letitia — no probs.
Gus You'll be terrific. Trust me.
Lenny Why is it, Dad, when you say "Trust me", I know we're in for a cock-up that goes off the Richter scale?
Gus The show has eleven million viewers.
Lenny Eleven million people watching me — eleven million. That's like everybody I've got in my whole address book and then ten million, nine hundred and ninety-nine thousand, nine hundred and forty-two *other* people — complete strangers, watching me.
Gus Calm down.
Lenny It's all getting out of hand. I can't go on. I mean how, how, how did we get into this?
Gus It wasn't *we*, it was you. You masquerading as a female novelist. You dressing up as that ghastly hideous woman and writing your daft slushy bloody awful books. Don't blame me.
Lenny You haven't done too badly out of it.
Gus Maybe not, but without me and Dee Dee you couldn't keep up the Myrtle charade, could you?
Lenny (*hurt*) Maybe not, but there's no need to make personal remarks. The *Daily Mail* said I was coquettish and delightfully feminine.
Gus With a telephoto lens the paparazzi would soon find you'd got one or two little secrets tucked away.
Lenny They'll hunt me down and beat me to pulp.
Gus Who?
Lenny The military wing of Mills and Boon. I could go to prison.
Gus What as?
Lenny I don't know. A gender bender offender.

Gus chuckles

What are you laughing at?
Gus I was just wondering how you'd cope with bathtime in Cell Block H.
Lenny It has got to stop. It can't go on. I've had enough. (*From the cupboard he produces a wig block dressed with Myrtle's accessories—the wig, plus full garish make-up, jewellery etc. He displays it to the others*) Look at her. The witch, she has taken over my life.
Gus There's a lot of women look much worse than that.
Lenny Such as?
Gus Clare Short, Esther Rantzen, Anne Widdecombe ...
Lenny I tell you, I am sick and tired of it all. The make-up, the jewellery, the high heels, the false tits ...
Gus You love it.

Act I

Lenny I do not. You try buying a nursing bra at Mothercare.
Gus Why Mothercare? What's wrong with Marks and Sparks?
Lenny I have trouble with the clasp at the back. I have to have a front loader.
Gus I reckon they're more fun on other people.
Dee Dee What?
Gus Tits. You should just be grateful Myrtle is so long in the tooth.
Lenny What do you mean?
Gus I think you'd find the full rumpity-pump a bit uncomfortable.
Lenny The mind boggles. I've only ever had a very basic grasp of the whole wretched sex business as it is.
Gus It's all my fault, Lenny. I thought they'd covered sex education in the second form.
Lenny They did. I was off having my verrucae done the afternoon they did reproduction. All you ever told me was to watch out for older boys offering me toffees in the playground.
Gus And here you are, East Twickenham's answer to Lily Savage. I should have given you a proper lecture with diagrams.
Dee Dee All you did for me was give me a book, "Breeding Among Primates" — written in 1904.
Lenny I don't expect they've changed mating habits much in the last hundred years. All I'm saying is I am sick and tired of Myrtle Bloody Banbury. I can't go on.
Dee Dee Dad, listen, you are a writer — you have used a pen name, that's all, an innocent little deception.
Lenny I tell you I am hoisted on my own leotard. I have cheated above and beyond the call of duty. I am the star writer of Love Is All Around, an exclusively feminist publishing house. Their motto is "For Women By Women".
Dee Dee So?
Lenny *I am a bloke*, my darling. A fraud. I could be unmasked, defrocked at any moment. I am living a lie. I mean I have just been voted Granny of the Year by the readers of "Knitting For Pleasure". I have danced a tango with Robert Kilroy Silk at a charity ball. I have even been paid to promote a product for the removal of unwanted hair. That made my eyes water.
Gus It's just as well you turned down that guest spot in *The Vagina Monologues* at Milton Keynes.
Lenny No really, I can't do it any more — I can't go on.

Lenny exits with the Myrtle wig block

Gus It's just stage fright. He's always been bashful.

Gus pours Dee Dee a glass of wine during the following

Dee Dee Poor Dad ... What's going to happen to him?
Gus When you fly the nest? It's a problem you're staring in the face a bit, isn't it?
Dee Dee What do you mean?
Gus (*giving her the drink*) You know what I mean, my darling, I am not stupid. Stupid about where I left my glasses and how to work the video and stuff but not about serious things ... I know what's going on.
Dee Dee Meaning?
Gus Come here.

Dee Dee goes to Gus. He hugs her

How far gone are you?
Dee Dee Meaning?
Gus When is the baby due?
Dee Dee (*after a beat*) April the seventeenth ... Oh Grampi — how did you know?
Gus I know the same way I know your father's athlete's foot is better.
Dee Dee How's that?
Gus (*tapping his nose*) The bathroom cupboard is a great oracle. It's not what people take from it that gives the game away — it's what they *stop* taking from it.
Dee Dee Got it.
Gus Exactly ... Lenny hasn't touched his foot powder for weeks.
Dee Dee I see.
Gus Plus I reckoned that if it was your father who'd bought the Predictor Kit from Boots he probably thought it was for the weather. Congratulations.
Dee Dee You're pleased?
Gus Oh yes. I love babies. Everything about them, even the nappies. I love it all — the talcum, the dribbling, the sleepless nights ...
Dee Dee Yeah, yeah — and that's just to get pregnant.
Gus Seriously, I do love babies. Well, not your father, of course — he was ghastly, a cross between Shrek and John Prescott.
Dee Dee Oh Grampi ...
Gus I shall be getting quite old of course, by the time it's ready to come to Highbury. I presume it is Justin's?
Dee Dee (*punching him*) Grampi ... .
Gus Does he know?

Dee Dee nods

What did he say?
Dee Dee He said, "Mine?" I said, "Yes." He said "A sprog?" I said "Yes." He said "Wow." He said "wow" seven times.

Act I

Gus He's always had a way with words.
Dee Dee He said "You can call it Mondeo."
Gus Mondeo?
Dee Dee His gran drives a Mondeo ——
Gus What's that got to do with ... ?
Dee Dee (*giving him a patient look*) — which Justin sometimes borrows at the weekend.
Gus Oh, I see ... Lucky it wasn't a BMW 7SL. So he's happy about it?
Dee Dee Up to a point. He wasn't sure what Mandy would make of it.
Gus Mandy?
Dee Dee His new girlfriend .... A junior stylist at Toni and Guy. All frizzy hair and too posh to wash.
Gus What a bummer. Are you all right?
Dee Dee Yes and no.
Gus Yes, you're fit and well. And no, how in hell are you going to tell your dad?
Dee Dee Exactly. His little girl having a baby.
Gus By a bloke with a pony tail, a tattoo, a nose ring, a Harley Davidson *and* a junior stylist at Toni and Guy. Remind me not to be anywhere this side of the equator when you tell him.
Dee Dee He's such a prude. Remember at my eighteenth disco party: we found him in the gallery crouching behind the glitter ball with his binoculars. He sent me a text message, "Dance more — snog less."
Gus He sent it to me too.
Dee Dee Then when he got the idea I'd had some body piercing done, he tried scanning me with his metal detector while I was watching telly. He's always hated me growing up.
Gus We had to buy your first bra by mail order.
Dee Dee Do you remember how upset he was when I found out about Father Christmas?
Gus (*nodding*) Have you told anyone else?
Dee Dee About Father Christmas? I wouldn't dream of it.
Gus Would you like *me* to tell him? I could do it really casually.
Dee Dee (*as Gus*) "Oh by the way, Lenny, Dee Dee's up the duff."
Gus Perhaps not. So, my pet, you're going to be a single parent, huh?
Dee Dee Seems to run in the family ... It's all pretty scary isn't it?
Gus Yeah. Well I'm told the actual birth business is a bit tricky, but then women have never been very good about pain.
Dee Dee (*hitting him hard*) Two pounds ...
Gus (*paying*) Ow. So I'm the first to know then?
Dee Dee I told Mum.
Gus Mum? Your mother? You told your mother?
Dee Dee Yes.
Gus You've seen her? Actually seen her? In the flesh?

Dee Dee Yes.

Gus Does your father know you've been seeing his ex-wife behind his back?

Dee Dee She wrote saying she wanted to see me. I thought why not? So I gave her a ring and fixed a date; she said "I'll be the one carrying a copy of *The Times*."

Gus How was she?

Dee Dee She was fine. Actually I think we were both pretty nervous. She gave me this T-shirt she'd had done — it said, "My mum ran off with an Italian and all I got was this lousy T-shirt."

Gus laughs, then looks puzzled

Gus I don't get it.

Dee Dee It was like a joke, Grampi, but also a kind of way of saying sorry for being pants as a mother.

Gus And you told her about the baby?

Dee Dee No, actually she told me. I said, "I've got something to tell you", and she said "Oh, so you're pregnant, then?"

Gus She never liked me, your mother — she even fixed the wedding for the Saturday Arsenal were playing away to Bolton Wanderers in the hope that I wouldn't be able to come.

Dee Dee That must have been a tricky call for you.

Gus It was — but I got back in time for the reception. Did she ask after me?

Dee Dee Yes. She said I don't suppose he's dead yet. Actually she was really keen to hear about Myrtle. It turns out she's a great fan of hers.

Gus (*laughing*) Oh that's just gorgeous ... You didn't tell her?

Dee Dee About Myrtle? Of course not. That's a secret the three of us are going to have to take to the grave.

Gus Here lies Gus Loftus the loving father of Twickenham's most famous transvestite.

Dee Dee She wanted to know how Dad felt about her.

Gus You didn't tell her that he's still got her photograph on his desk and that on their anniversary he sits in a darkened room with a packet of Liquorice Allsorts and plays all her old Elvis albums.

Dee Dee Poor old Dad.

Gus As he says, it's not much fun being a Darby when your Joan has done a runner.

Dee Dee No. Was Mum always big on Elvis by the way? Let's hope that's not a genetic problem.

Dee Dee exits

Gus (*as if he is a TV reporter talking to a camera*) And now, on that bombshell, back to the studio. This is Gus Loftus in Twickenham.

Act I

Lenny enters the basement study, rehearsing with some cue cards

Lenny (*to himself*) Hi, there, I am Leonard — call me Lenny — Loftus. An ordinary b ... b ... bloke leading an ordinary l ... l ... life ... .

Dee Dee enters carrying a small box

Dee Dee How's it going?
Lenny Not very well.
Dee Dee Right. On we go. I'm going to be Letitia, OK? (*She moves the chairs into a suitable arrangement for an interview*)
Lenny OK.
Dee Dee Right. We're all set. Sit. We are rehearsing, right?
Lenny Right.
Dee Dee The camera is up there on the wall now. OK?
Lenny OK.
Dee Dee They are letting us practise with it before tomorrow; it's rigged so we can see it upstairs on the laptop, OK? We are not yet linked up to the actual studio. It's like CCTV. Do you understand? Tell me you understand.
Lenny I understand.
Dee Dee Do you really?
Lenny No.
Dee Dee The camera is there — use it. And cue ... Go on ... . (*She points to the centre of the fourth wall*)
Lenny Hi, there, yes I am L ... L ... Leonard — call me Lenny — Loftus. An ordinary b ... b ... bloke ... . (*Giving up*) I can't do it, darling. My teeth have gone all dry.
Dee Dee Course you can. What song are you using at the moment?
Lenny For my cantartherapy? I've given up on *Somewhere Over The Rainbow*. Dr Frankleman wants me to try *Men of Harlech*.
Dee Dee (*to the tune of "Men of Harlech"*) I am Leonard, call me Lenny ...
Lenny (*singing too*) I am just a total prat ... (*Speaking*) This is no time for therapy.

Gus enters the living-room. He looks at the laptop screen and then thumps the floor. Dee Dee goes to the intercom

Dee Dee (*into the intercom*) Hi Grampi ... Can you see us on the monitor?
Gus (*into the intercom*) I can see you loud and clear. The thing is, Lenny, keep it loosey goosey.
Dee Dee (*to Lenny*) Here we go. Put this earpiece in. (*She produces a tiny (as good as invisible) earpiece from the box and gives it to Lenny*)
Lenny Where do I put it?

Dee Dee (*patiently*) It's an earpiece, Dad. You put it in your ear. No-one will see it, but through it you will be able to hear us guiding you if need be. OK?
Lenny Where'd you get it from, for God's sake?
Dee Dee Grampi used it on a clairvoyant scam we tried. Plus you've got all the notes. Now come on, put it in.

Lenny puts in the earpiece

OK?
Lenny Testing, testing ... .
Dee Dee (*on the intercom*) Grampi. Pick up the microphone.
Lenny Come in Houston ... Mary had a little lamb ...

Gus picks up the small microphone on the desk to reply. NB: Again we just accept that the earpiece is working

Gus (*into the microphone*) And the midwife called it Baaaasil.
Lenny Ha ha. It's working.
Gus (*into the microphone; Germanically*) Vorsprung durch Technik.
Lenny (*to the camera*) You're a dirty old man, Dad, not an Audi Automatic.
Dee Dee All set then? Are you happy?
Lenny Happy? Not even close.
Dee Dee (*in a severe tone*) So Lenny, tell me about yourself.
Lenny I beg your pardon?
Dee Dee I'm being Letitia, OK?
Lenny (*stupidly*) If you're being Letitia, darling, where are you, Dee Dee?
Dee Dee Dad, I will be upstairs with Grampi watching you. OK?
Lenny What about Myrtle, where's she?
Dee Dee Myrtle doesn't exist, Dad. She's away — abroad. OK? (*Again in the tone of Letitia*) So, Lenny, tell me about yourself.
Lenny Right. And I say ... .
Gus (*into the microphone*) It's on the card, you prat.
Lenny It's on the card ... Oh yes. (*Reading his cue card*) "Well I'm just a boring old statistician, Letitia, a single parent waiting for Miss Right to come along." I can't say this.
Dee Dee Yes, you can — go on.
Lenny (*giving up*) But, darling, I'm not waiting for Miss Right to come along. She's been and gone. She came along and then she buggered off.
Dee Dee Come on, there have been others.
Lenny Not really, your mum was something a bit special. (*He holds up the photograph*) The rest are just like taxis on a wet evening — they're either busy or going the other way. I'm sick of getting splashed as they pass.
Dee Dee Oh, Dad, get a grip — move on.

Act I

Lenny I've tried—I can't. Not really. It's a bit like sciatica. A dull ache with the odd twinge.
Dee Dee Take a Paracetamol. Come on ... Back to work: (*as Letitia again*) Now, Lenny, tell me a bit about your family life.
Lenny (*looking at his notes*) Well, my daughter Dee Dee is about to go to Exeter University, and my father who is — fifty-nine ... (*To the camera*) Fifty-nine!
Gus (*into the microphone*) Picky picky picky ... All right then — sixty-one.
Lenny Sixty-one ... He is amusing and erudite with ... (*peering at the handwriting*) a cranberry preserve.
Gus (*into the microphone*) Charismatic personality — whom women find strangely attractive.
Lenny (*to Dee Dee*) He's a bloody liability. I just found his Arsenal knickers in with my all whites ... .
Dee Dee (*suddenly not well*) On, on, Dad.
Lenny You know Letitia, I think he'd make great TV sports presenter.
Dee Dee (*with her hand to her mouth*) Excuse me a moment, I think I'm going to be ... (*She moves to the stairs*)
Lenny Oh my God. Are you all right, darling?
Dee Dee Yeah, probably something I've eaten.

Dee Dee exits up the stairs

Lenny (*to Gus*) That'll be your seafood risotto, I expect.

The doorbell of the upper front door rings. Gus answers the entryphone

Lenny works at his desk during the following

Gus (*into the entryphone*) Hallo. Yes.
Fran (*voice-over*) Is that Gus Loftus Enterprises?
Gus (*into the entryphone; worried*) Why do you ask?
Fran (*voice-over*) It's what's marked on the bell, Gus.
Gus Yes, it is I. Me. This is them. Is that who I think it is?
Fran (*voice-over*) How should I know. It's me, Fran Loftus. Your ex-daughter-in-law. Let me in will you, Gus?

Gus presses the door release

Gus (*to himself, out front*) "The following scene may contain violence and explicit language."

Fran enters the living-room. She has a handbag with her

Gus holds the door

Hallo Frannie — it's been quite a while.
Fran It has indeed.
Gus Lenny's not here, I'm afraid.

Gus stamps on the floor. Fran looks at him

What can I offer you?
Fran Nothing thanks. So you're still in residence, Gus?
Gus Yes.
Fran After all these years?
Gus So it would seem.
Fran Like a moth in a cashmere warehouse. Nice place.
Gus Yes.
Fran So Lenny's not here?
Gus No.
Fran (*looking at the laptop screen*) What's this then?
Gus A screen saver. (*He stamps urgently*)

Lenny looks up from his work

Lenny (*unaware the microphone is still live*) Shut up.

Fran and Gus react to this

Gus (*copying Lenny's tone*) Shut up — the laptop by closing the lid. There we are. (*He shuts the laptop lid*)
Fran Very hi-tech.
Gus So you've just got back from Italy, have you?
Fran Yes.
Gus On your broomstick?
Fran Nice one. It's amazing really.
Gus What?
Fran That you managed to grow old without actually growing up.
Gus No trouble like that with you and your toy-boy, I expect?
Fran We never even pretended to like one another, did we?
Gus (*charmingly*) No — what was the point? I did my best at your engagement party, extending the hand of friendship and all that.
Fran My father had to throw you out in the street.
Gus Yeah, the plonker, he got his knickers well and truly twisted.
Fran As to what you were doing in the tool shed with my mother ...

Gus stamps on the floor again, more urgently

Act I   15

Gus I was trying to cheer her up.
Fran By putting your hand of friendship up her skirt.

Lenny reacts to the thumping on his ceiling. He hits the ceiling with his broom handle. There is an obvious rhythm so Gus answers with a flourish of flamenco-like stamping to cover it

Gus *Olé!*
Fran Do I get the feeling you don't want me to see Lenny?
Gus It's not really any of my business.
Fran That never used to stop you.
Gus *(pointing the way)* Through there and down the stairs.
Fran You haven't changed, Gus.
Gus Thank you.
Fran It wasn't actually meant as a compliment, Gus.

Fran exits

Gus Of course not; silly me. *(He quickly opens the laptop and picks up the microphone. Into the microphone)* Will Leonard Loftus please come to the Diary Room immediately?
Lenny *(hearing via his earpiece)* Yes?
Gus *(into the microphone)* Fran is here.
Lenny *(as if electrocuted)* Fran? My Fran? I mean Fran — here? Upstairs?
Gus *(into the microphone)* On her way down; she should be with you on the count of three — one two three.

Fran enters the study. Lenny quickly conceals the photograph of Fran on his desk and stands

Fran Hallo.
Lenny Hallo.

They just stand facing one another

Dee Dee enters the living-room

Dee Dee Is that Mum's car ... ?
Gus Sssssh. *(He signals her to watch her parents on the screen with him)*
Dee Dee Oh my God ... What is going on down there?
Gus Ssssh. I'm timing them. It could be one of the longest nastiest pauses in history.

The pause goes on

Oh, yes — this is one that Pinter could be proud of.
Dee Dee It can't go on.
Gus I don't think he'd be much good at speed-dating.
Dee Dee Is his earpiece still in? (*She picks up the microphone and taps it*)

Lenny jumps

(*Into the microphone*) Dad, take a deep breath.

Lenny takes a deep breath

Relax your shoulders.

Lenny's shoulders drop

Say something.
Lenny Something.
Fran What?
Lenny Hallo.
Fran We've done that.
Dee Dee (*into the microphone*) Shall we try: how are you?
Lenny How are you?
Fran I'm fine thank you. And you?
Lenny (*to the camera*) How am I?
Dee Dee (*into the microphone*) You're fine too.
Lenny I'm fine too.
Dee Dee (*into the microphone*) How about the weather?
Lenny How about the weather?
Fran Horrible. You don't seem very pleased to see me.
Dee Dee (*into the microphone*) Are you OK?
Lenny No.
Fran I see.
Lenny (*confused*) No, I mean ... .
Dee Dee (*into the microphone*) Do you want me to come down?
Lenny No. I mean yes.
Fran Yes. There's more rain due apparently.

Dee Dee exits down the stairs

Gus (*picking up the microphone; into his son's ear*) Why don't you take off all your clothes and do a tap dance?

Act I

Lenny Why don't you ... ? (*He looks venomously at the camera*)

Dee Dee enters the study. She sees the awkwardness of Lenny and Fran

Dee Dee Well, isn't this nice. The two of you here like this. (*To Fran*) Hm?
Fran Yes.
Dee Dee (*to Lenny*) Hm?
Lenny Yes.

Dee Dee watches them both for a moment

Dee Dee "The person you're calling knows you are waiting, please stay on the line." (*Prompting Lenny*) Would you like a drink?
Lenny Would you like a drink?
Fran No, thank you.
Dee Dee These are my goldfish. Dreadnought and Marigold.
Lenny These are my goldfish. Dreadnought and Marigold.
Fran Lovely. Which is which?
Lenny Dreadnought is the male.

Pause

Dee Dee Well look at the pair of you chatting away ... I've got to go. I'll see you later. You've got my mobile number, haven't you, Mum?
Fran (*kissing Dee Dee*) Sure. I'll call you.

Unseen by Lenny, Dee Dee puts her finger to her lips then mimes cradling a baby—i.e. telling Mum to keep mum. Lenny turns to catch the end of this and Dee Dee quickly changes the rocking of a baby to an exaggerated dance (the Twist)

Dee Dee It's making a come-back. (*Kissing Lenny*) Bye Dad.

Lenny is stupefied

(*Speaking for him*) Goodbye Dee Dee, darling. Have you got enough money, darling? Here take a tenner from my wallet, why don't you? Oh no I couldn't. I insist. Oh all right. (*She takes his wallet from the desk drawer and removes a tenner*) Thanks, Dad.

Dee Dee exits

Lenny (*realizing he's been duped*) Hey ... .

But Dee Dee has gone. There is more silence between Lenny and Fran

Gus (*into the microphone*) I'd do your flies up if I were you.

Lenny reacts instinctively

Got you.

Gus closes the laptop and exits, chuckling

Fran Awkward, huh?
Lenny No.
Fran Suit yourself.
Lenny (*after a moment*) OK — it's awkward.
Fran What's that thing in your ear?
Lenny (*taking out the earpiece*) It's invisible.
Fran Obviously. Are you going to ask me to sit down?
Lenny (*sitting*) Won't you sit down?
Fran No thanks. I'm better standing for awkward.
Lenny (*rising again*) Then we'll both stand.
Fran I suppose there are two ways of doing this.
Lenny This what?
Fran The conversation thing. We can go the frosty formal route or we could try being a tad more *Sex and the City* about it.
Lenny How would that be?
Fran Well, we could do the "Wow, you haven't changed a bit, so what do you make of New Labour, what car are you driving, how's the old dandruff problem, yes, thanks, I'd love a glass of chardonnay," type of thing.
Lenny I do not have dandruff. (*Pause*) If it's OK with you I'd be happier with the frosty formal option.
Fran That wouldn't be the Myrtle choice.
Lenny Let's just keep her out of this.
Fran I'm so sad I never met her. How come she didn't come to our wedding?
Lenny She was in ... She was in — re-hab.
Fran Re-hab? Poor woman. So, she took after her brother then.
Lenny Her brother?
Fran Your father.
Lenny No, no. On my mother's side. He's my mother's sister. She's my mother's brother. Sister. She. Myrtle is my mother's sister.
Fran You always said your mother was an only child.
Lenny Er, no — not only — *lonely*. She was a lonely child.
Fran Ah. So what was she into — drugs, booze?
Lenny Yes. She was snorting a lot of glue.

Act I

Fran Glue?
Lenny Yes.
Fran You don't snort glue. You sniff glue. You snort coke.
Lenny There you are — she was too pissed to notice.
Fran She's a beautiful woman. Such style and class.
Lenny Thank you ... Yes, absolutely.
Fran Why do you suppose she took so against you, then?
Lenny What do you mean? She loves me.
Fran I have noticed there's no record of the two of you ever having been seen together in public.
Lenny That's true.
Fran Lots of photographs of her and that filthy old sleaze-bag your father but none of you and her together. There wasn't anything going on between them, was there?
Lenny Going on?
Fran You know — a thing.
Lenny A thing? You mean a thing thing? Between Dad and Aunt Myrtle?
Fran Yes.
Lenny It's an interesting question. But the words "very long barge-pole" and "hell freezing over" are involved in the answer. Dad's not her type.
Fran What do you know?
Lenny I know a racing cert when I see it.
Fran She's a woman with balls.
Lenny That's part of the trouble.
Fran Her books have given me the strength to be independent, to be the me I am now.
Lenny Well, isn't life full of little ironies?
Fran I don't expect you to understand — it's a woman thing. Still, I suppose Myrtle's made you all rich — I don't imagine you have to work much nowadays.
Lenny Look, is there something you want from me?
Fran The words "very long barge-pole" and "hell freezing over" ... There's no need to panic, Lenny.
Lenny I'm sorry.
Fran Your stuttering has improved.
Lenny Thank you.
Fran You used to do it when you were aroused.
Lenny Yes. Precisely.
Fran Not any more then? You're cured.
Lenny Not necessarily.
Fran Touché. Have I aged so badly?
Lenny To be honest, hardly at all.
Fran When you first asked me up to your flat the word "coffee" took you three minutes.

Lenny It wasn't instant.
Fran Boom boom. And your proposal was irresistible – "Will you m-m-m-mmmm ... ?"
Lenny I was trying to say "manage without me".
Fran That's not true either. You loved me, there's no reason to be ashamed of that.
Lenny I didn't say I was ashamed. Getting married is a high risk business, we all know that. A bit like pyramid selling.
Fran In what way?
Lenny It works very well for some people — other poor suckers get shafted.
Fran Dee Dee tells me you've been having speech therapy.
Lenny It's called *cantartherapy*. It's a Californian idea. You have to sing the words that you find difficult.
Fran But you can't sing.
Lenny Oh damn, I should have thought of that. You pick a song you know and then you just put in the words you want to say.
Fran What's your song?
Lenny It varies. On a good day it's "Old MacDonald had a farm".
Fran And on a bad one?
Lenny "It's my party and I'll cry if I want to".
Fran Show me how that works.
Lenny No. It's private.
Fran Mine would have to be an Elvis song, I suppose. Have you still got all my albums?
Lenny I'm not sure. I might have somewhere.
Fran Thanks ... Please don't imagine this is easy for me.
Lenny You always liked a challenge.
Fran You probably think I'm looking for some kind of truce. I mean all the angst is sort of past its sell-by date now, isn't it? Water under the bridge.
Lenny I don't know.
Fran What's it been — nine years since we separated?
Lenny Eight years ... Six months ... Two weeks.
Fran Not that you're counting. Doesn't time fly?
Lenny No, it doesn't actually. And we didn't separate. You left.
Fran Same difference. We split.
Lenny No. It's not the same difference. You left. I stayed. I am still here. I never moved. I never separated.
Fran Whatever ...
Lenny It's — like saying William the Conqueror never won the Battle of Hastings, Harold just said "Oh, dear, look, I've got a dirty great arrow stuck in my eye, why don't you just move in to my country and be king ... "
Fran So your point is?
Lenny You can't re-write history.

Fran The past is that way, the future this. Lenny, let it go.

Lenny produces a letter from the desk

Lenny (*reading*) "Dear Lenny, I am leaving you. I am staying here in Italy, I have found somebody else. I know this will be difficult for you and I'm sorry——"
Fran Don't do this, Lenny.
Lenny (*reading*) "— we have grown apart. It's not our fault we are incompatible. All in all, a clean break is for the best. Perhaps you should get your father to come over to help out for a few days ..." (*To Fran*) I wish I could find the words to thank you for that suggestion. (*Reading*) "You are a dear kind man, take care of yourself. Fran."
Fran Is that all?
Lenny (*reading*) "PS I've taken all my things; could you look after my Elvis albums. Ta."
Fran Nothing about Dee Dee?
Lenny (*he knows this by heart*) "PPS I'll leave it to you to explain to Dee Dee. I'm sure she'll understand."
Fran Do you think she did?
Lenny Oh, yes — she said she didn't really mind my being so boring.
Fran Do you think that we can move on ... To try and find ...
Lenny Uh-ho ... Please don't ...
Fran What?
Lenny You were going to use the word "closure" weren't you?
Fran Why not?
Lenny Closure applies to schools and factories and surgical wounds and maybe one day, who knows, *The Mousetrap*. Closure has nothing to do with people's feelings. It's just a cliché. It has no emotional weight. Closure, bah ... .
Fran (*mocking*) Closure — bah! You're right, it's bland. I just thought there was an outside chance that we could — be friends.
Lenny Exchange Christmas cards you mean?
Fran I think Dee Dee would appreciate it.
Lenny You don't think you've left the maternal side of things a bit late — Dee Dee is grown up.
Fran Yeah. I noticed. Very nicely too. She's fantastic. Well-balanced, funny, kind.
Lenny Well, that's the luck of the draw with the gene pool, isn't it? You've been seeing her then, I gather?
Fran We had lunch. I wrote her a letter. I was so nervous, isn't it ridiculous. You must be very proud. Note I said "you" not "we" — I take no credit in that department.

Lenny She's your daughter too.
Fran (*unable to tell Lenny about Dee Dee's baby*) Yeah. Well, who's to say when a girl might need her mum?
Lenny Yea. There were times when it would have been easier if she had been a boy. I mean, you know, bathroom-wise. All that puberty thing was a bit tricky. Suddenly down came all the My Little Pony posters and up went Wet Wet Wet and Johnny Depp. Just like that. Dad called it "the three Ts years".
Fran The three Ts?
Lenny Tits, tampons and tantrums. We collected over six thousand air miles at Boots. She was like a cross between Christine Hamilton and Donald Rumsfeld. She's quite like you in that area.
Fran I'll take that as a compliment.
Lenny Yes. I've still got the scar from when you threw the wok at me.
Fran Thank God for Aunt Myrtle then.
Lenny What do you mean?
Fran At least she had Myrtle as a role model to teach her about things.
Lenny What things?
Fran Girl things.
Lenny Oh those. Yes, well, Dad knows the ropes pretty well. Between us we m-m-mmm ...
Fran Muddled through?
Lenny Thank you.
Fran She has a boyfriend, I gather.
Lenny Not really. He's a bit of a lout. I don't think it's anything serious.
Fran No?
Lenny No.
Fran You don't think they're sleeping together, then?
Lenny Oh please. Of course not. Is it likely?
Fran Aaah ...
Lenny For heaven's sake. He's not the type. He hasn't even got a car.
Fran You don't have to have a driving licence to shag, you know.
Lenny Or an MOT in my case. No, I keep a good eye on her; she never stays out — she's either here or with Melanie.
Fran Melanie?
Lenny Her friend.
Fran Yes, of course. So Myrtle never recommended she go on the Pill, then?
Lenny Pill. What pill? ... The Pill. Look have you just come here to try and make trouble ... The Pill ... Tsk ...
Fran That's "tsk" is it? A "bah" and a "tsk". Are you turning into a boring old fart?
Lenny It wouldn't be surprising — I was a young one for long enough. No. The point is Dee Dee is — is ... .

Act I

Fran What? What is she, Lenny?
Lenny (*facing the abyss*) She's a girl.
Fran A woman.
Lenny Yes — well, a kind of trainee. We'll cross that bridge when we come to it. Look, what is the exact purpose of this visit?
Fran (*producing a big packet of Liquorice Allsorts and tossing it to Lenny*) I brought you these.
Lenny Thanks.
Fran A peace offering. The orange ones, right?
Lenny (*nodding*) Pink coconut — you.
Fran Yeah. Plus I was sure you'd have one of your statistics for me.
Lenny I haven't. You never liked statistics anyway ... Is that all?
Fran Not really. I'm getting married.
Lenny (*after a long pause*) In the UK we eat half a million kilos of sausages a day. Allowing that you get twelve sausages to the kilo and that each sausage is four inches long that means we eat three hundred and seventy-eight point eight-seven miles of sausages every day.
Fran That's a lot of sausages.
Lenny Enough to go three times round the M25.
Fran Somebody actually paid you to work that out?
Lenny No, I did that for fun ... To what's-his-name?
Fran Luigi Deparuvia. We fly out to Barbados next week.
Lenny You're getting married in Barbados?
Fran Yes. With a calypso band, on the beach. It's the full moon.
Lenny Too much information.
Fran I'm wearing a lime green organza dress, if you want to know.
Lenny I don't. I don't. I don't need the details. (*Pause*) Lime green. I hope you'll be very happy.
Fran Do you mean that?
Lenny Of course not.
Fran It didn't work out for you then? With ... ?
Lenny What's-her-name.
Fran Your aunt's publisher at Love Is All Around.
Lenny Harriet Copeland. No, it didn't work out with Harriet Copeland.
Fran The old drift-apart syndrome?
Lenny She dumped me. Said she wanted more space. More space for her twenty-six year-old Puerto Rican fitness trainer.
Fran I'm sorry.
Lenny Yes it was a p-p ...
Fran Pisser.
Lenny I was going to say pity.
Fran So you're on your own then?
Lenny Yup.

Fran Celibate?
Lenny Yup. Mind you, the goldfish keep me pretty busy.
Fran Get a life, Lenny.
Lenny Goldfish have one great advantage, you know, when it comes to reproduction — they don't have to actually meet to procreate. They make their contribution independently.
Fran A bit like the royal family, I imagine. What you're saying is, you're afraid of being hurt.
Lenny Er ... Look ... I voted for formal and frosty — you want closure. I hope the wedding goes well — on the beach in Bermuda under the full moon. Thanks for the Liquorice Allsorts. I wish you and Luigi every happiness.
Fran Barbados. That was very nice, Lenny. I hope you find happiness too.
Lenny Thank you.
Fran I'll be off then. Send my love to Dee Dee. Don't you worry about her growing up too fast.
Lenny I wasn't. Should I?
Fran No, of course not, but just in case. (*Moving to the doorway*) I got that bit right anyway — It's not our fault we're incompatible.
Lenny It only takes one to be incompatible.
Fran Yeah ... Well, see you around, Lenny.

They hesitate; how to say good-bye?

Fran Do we kiss or shake hands?
Lenny How about we sort of raise a non-committal hand?
Fran Right.

They each raise a non-committal hand

Fran exits. Lenny exits with the Liquorice Allsorts to the kitchen

The doorbell of the upper front door rings

Gus enters the living-room

Gus And next, folks, a plague of locusts. Oh ... (*He opens the door*)

Letitia Butters is revealed in the doorway. She is an impressive-looking woman, flamboyantly dressed, with dark glasses. She is very theatrical — her mood and tone change often, switching from kitten to tiger, from melodrama to mysticism, etc.

Act I

Letitia Letitia Butters. "Mind Your Own Business".
Gus I thought you weren't coming until tomorrow.
Letitia Did you indeed?
Gus Yes, tomorrow — Thursday.
Letitia Tomorrow is Friday.
Gus Yesterday wasn't Wednesday.
Letitia I'm afraid it was. Yesterday was Wednesday. Tomorrow is Friday. Today is, ergo, Thursday.
Gus I seem to have lost Tuesday. Come in, how do you do?

Letitia enters fully

Letitia You must be Gus Loftus, Myrtle's nephew's father.
Gus That's right. It's an honour to meet you.
Letitia Of course it is. How do you do? I was expecting a much older man.
Gus Well, I've looked after myself.
Letitia That's what I heard.

They shake hands. Gus is in awe

Letitia (*taking off her sunglasses*) Call me Letish. A good steady hand and positive eye contact. That's what I like in a man.
Gus I'm so glad. I'm a big fan of yours, actually, from way back ...
Letitia (*stopping him*) Ssssh ... Don't move. Apricot.
Gus Apricot?
Letitia That's what I'm getting from you — apricot. That's your aura.
Gus That's good, is it?
Letitia No. It speaks to me of indecision and vacillation. (*She studies him*) You need more root vegetables. Do you get enough fresh air?
Gus Well, I seem to get by.
Letitia I speak as I find, Gus. I have powers. I am aware of things.
Gus Obviously. Was this a talent you were born with?
Letitia Even as a baby. I've nurtured it of course. I've honed my skills. Voices from the past, glimpses of the future ... I'm a conduit, do you understand?
Gus I do. And you think I need more root vegetables?
Letitia I'm not infallible, Gus. Are you bisexual?
Gus Absolutely not. I don't even watch Graham Norton any more.
Letitia It was just a thought. Apricot nevertheless. You were saying? (*She explores the living room during the following*)
Gus I was just saying — how much I used to enjoy your weather forecasts. Oh yes. Yes, yes, yes. Nobody did a belt of rain moving in from the Atlantic better than you.

Letitia You liked my presentation?
Gus (*full of happy memories*) Oh, yes, I couldn't get enough of your bad weather first thing in the morning. None of us could.
Letitia None of you?
Gus In the barracks at Brize Norton. Lovely jubbly.
Letitia (*sensually*) Especially up over the North of Scotland and The Hebrides eh? (*She erotically mimes moving weather symbols over Scotland*)
Gus Absolutely.
Letitia My breasts brushing gently against the East Midlands.
Gus Lucky old Birmingham.
Letitia Oh yes. My fan mail was always huge during periods of low pressure. So — you find me attractive then, Gus? Is that what you are subtly trying to imply?
Gus Well, I ... er ... .
Letitia I pick up on these things, these innuendoes. I'm fey, you see. I have the inner ear.
Gus And the outer mouth.
Letitia Do I frighten you, Gus?
Gus Good Lord, no. You are talking to a man who can watch the whole of *The Exorcist* alone in a darkened room.
Letitia You know, Gus, things can get pretty fruity at the cutting edge of reality TV. Life in the media glare can be solitary.
Gus Of course — I often worry about Anne Robinson.
Letitia *Don't*. For my public I'm Letitia Butters the icon of thrusting reality TV, but underneath, Gus, I'm a little furry bunny.
Gus A little furry bunny.

They are entranced with each other

Letitia (*pulling herself together*) So now, are you all set for the video diary?
Gus I'm looking forward to it.
Letitia Is the camera installed yet?
Gus Yes, in the study downstairs. They're hooking us up to the studio tomorrow, I think. You know, Letitia, I'd like to be in the media.
Letitia What as?
Gus I could be sort of a front man for the barmy army. (*As a fruity reporter*) "And now back to the studio. This is Gus Loftus — for *News at Ten* — at the mud-wrestling contest in Marbella."
Letitia Yes, you may have got something.
Gus People tell me I'm quite loosey goosey.
Letitia Do they? Well, I'll certainly try to get you embedded somewhere.
Gus Will you?

Act I

Letitia (*enamoured*) We could give it a whirl. Can I be frank with you?
Gus Oh yes. Carry on.
Letitia I really really need to speak to Myrtle. You must know where to find her, Gus, a man in your position ...
Gus Of course I do. But I told you I cannot give you her number. We did make it clear that Myrtle's privacy had to be respected.
Letitia (*seductively steely*) So what? Call Myrtle for me, Gus.
Gus He wouldn't like it. *She*. She wouldn't like it. Not at all. I mean she'd be furious. She's a recluse — miles away — up the Amazon in the rainforest for instance, at the moment.
Letitia (*handing Gus the telephone; as a dominatrix*) Dial her number, Gus. Dial it for me, Gus. Go on ...

Gus dials, beguiled by Letitia

In the study, the special pink telephone rings in the desk drawer

Dee Dee runs on down the stairs

Lenny (*off*) Dee Dee — it's the Myrtle mobile!

Lenny enters from the kitchen

Dee Dee What? The hot line — it can't be.
Lenny Where the hell is Myrtle supposed to be at the moment? (*He takes the special pink telephone from a desk drawer*)

Dee Dee consults a chart

Dee Dee She's in ... She's in the Antarctic Ocean.
Lenny Are you sure?
Dee Dee Yes, yes. Cue six.

Lenny presses "Cue six" on his laptop. We hear the soundtrack of a ferocious ocean storm. Lenny clears his throat

Lenny (*into the phone; as Myrtle*) Hallo ... Hallo ... Myrtle Banbury here. Hallo.

Gus hands over the telephone to Letitia. The following conversation takes place over the telephone

Letitia Is that really you, Myrtle?

Lenny turns up the sea sound effects

Lenny Oh yes, it's really me Myrtle ... Who is this?
Letitia Letitia Butters. "Mind Your Own Business".
Lenny And the same to you with brass knobs on.
Letitia Where are you, my dear?
Lenny The Antarctic. I'm just rounding the Horn. (*An aside to the bosun*) Batten down the hatches, my hearties.
Letitia I thought you were in the rainforest, up the Amazon.
Lenny Did you? Was I? I'm up the Amazon am I? ... (*To Dee Dee, as himself, in a panic*) I'm up the Amazon. I'm up the Amazon, for God's sake.
Dee Dee Bumholes. Sorry Dad. (*Checking her chart*) Here we are ... Cue nine. Press cue nine.

Lenny presses another key. Instantly we hear farmyard noises and a cow's long "moooo"

Lenny (*as Myrtle*) There we are. What ... ?
Dee Dee Whoops. No. Cue seven, Dad, sorry, cue seven ...

Lenny hits another key. We hear the correct rain forest sound effects

Lenny Yes, yes here I am up the Amazon, I've just arrived — I came via Ambridge ... I've just landed. It's been a long day. My sea-legs are a bit wobbly ... How are you?
Letitia I'm fine. And you, Myrtle?
Lenny Tickety-boo. Look here I'm supposed to be incommunicado at the moment, Letitia ... .

On the sound track there is the loud laughing sound of a monkey

Lenny We're shooting a PG tips commercial. And you're in dear old Blighty, are you?
Letitia As a matter of fact I'm at Gus's office in Twickenham.
Lenny Oh-ho, are you indeed? (*To Dee Dee, as himself*) She's upstairs, the witch. She's with Dad ...
Letitia He's right here beside me.
Lenny (*as Myrtle*) You give him a great big kiss from me. What can I do for you?
Letitia Myrtle, I *must* have you on my show ... Must must must.
Lenny Oh no, no, no — Lenny can do it.
Letitia No, I want you both. I want you and Lenny together. All three of us chatting away, live as it were, here chez vous.

Act I

Lenny (*with false laughter*) Oh Letitia, you're pulling my pudding.
Letitia Certainly not. I'm quite serious.
Lenny You want me talking to Myrtle. I mean me talking to Lenny. Both of us. Together. Live — on your show.
Letitia Yes. It'll be a wow.
Lenny Yes. The thing is, Lenny and I are not really on speaking terms at the moment. He's a lovely boy of course, but he's become so ...
Dee Dee Mean and resentful.
Lenny (*fleetingly outraged*) Mean and ... Yes, he's become so mean and resentful.
Letitia Oh dear. Gus never said anything about a feud. We just thought having you on the show would be the icing on the cake.
Lenny Did you indeed? It was Gus's idea was it? Would you just put him on the line a moment?
Letitia (*passing the telephone to Gus*) She wants to talk to you.
Gus (*into the phone with bravura*) Hallo Myrtle, dear. Every thing all right up there in the rain forest?
Lenny Now listen here, you scheming Jurassic old scumbag — this is a "no-no". Do you hear me? A "no-no".
Gus (*ignoring him*) Oh, that's marvellous. Myrtle you are such a sport.
Lenny I am going to kill you, do hear me?
Gus Don't you worry, Myrtle, we'll get you a lovely new dress, something really gorgeous to show off your figure.
Lenny Listen here, I am going to cut up your Arsenal season ticket, Dad, and insert it forcefully piece by piece up your ——
Gus Hasta la vista, Myrtle ... .
Lenny Be afraid, Dad, be very afraid.

There is a knock on the upper front door

Gus (*into the telephone*) Hang on, Myrtle, there's someone at the door.

Gus lets Fran in. He keeps the telephone in his hand

Fran I forgot to collect my Elvis albums.
Gus Letitia Butters, this is Lenny's former wife, Francis Sutherland.
Fran Not *the* Letitia Butters?
Letitia Sadly there's only the one of me.
Gus (*into the telephone*) Guess what, Myrtle?
Lenny (*into his telephone, as himself*) Surprise me.
Gus Fran has just come in.
Lenny Fran?
Gus Yup. Isn't that nice?
Lenny Get rid of her. (*To Dee Dee*) Your mum is upstairs. I need a brandy.

Dee Dee exits

Gus (*to Fran*) Myrtle says "Hi there" from up the Amazon.
Fran I am such a big fan of hers.
Gus (*holding out the telephone*) Look, why don't you tell her yourself?
Fran Oh yes ... .
Gus (*into the telephone*) Here she is. Myrtle this is Fran, Fran this is Myrtle.
(*He gleefully passes the telephone to Fran*)
Lenny No, no, no ... Absolu ... .
Fran (*into the telephone*) Hallo.
Lenny (*quickly reverting to Myrtle's voice*) Hallo there.
Fran How do you do?
Lenny How do you do too?
Fran Me talking to you. Amazing. How about that?
Lenny It's too too exciting.
Fran Dee Dee has given me a proof copy of your new book.
Lenny Oh, did she? Bless her. Enjoy.
Fran She's a lovely girl, your niece.
Lenny Great, actually.
Fran Yes, indeed.
Lenny No — great-niece.
Letitia (*to Gus*) See me out, will you?
Fran (*into the telephone*) Hold on, Myrtle.
Letitia I'm going to Hell's Kitchen for dinner with little Gordon Ramsay.
(*To Fran*) Bye my dear.
Fran Goodbye.
Letitia (*peering at Gus*) Are you all right, Gus? Suddenly I'm getting brown — dark brown, all over.
Gus (*to Fran*) No change there, then.

Letitia exits followed by Gus

Lenny (*into the phone*) So what brings you back to England my dear?
Fran (*into the phone*) Lenny has been looking after my Elvis collection.
Lenny (*singing*) "Return to sender." (*Speaking*) Well, it's good to meet you at last. I've heard so much about you from Dee Dee and Gus.
Fran And from Lenny?
Lenny Yes. And from Lenny of course. I was to sorry not to have met you all those years ago. I was ... I was ...
Fran In re-hab.
Lenny Yes, I was a bit of a silly-billy — I'd been snorting when I should have been sniffing. Imagine. All bunged up with glue.
Fran You can't think very much of me.

Act I

Lenny What makes you say that, my dear?
Fran Well ... You know ... My walking out on Lenny like that.
Lenny Yes, I suppose it did put him off his Weetabix for a while. So you're getting married again.
Fran Yes.
Lenny In Bermuda.
Fran Barbados.
Lenny To an Italian?
Fran Yes.
Lenny Never mind. I'm surprised Dee Dee isn't going to be there for the big day?
Fran Probably not a good idea really — considering.
Lenny Considering what?
Fran You know what.
Lenny No. What?
Fran I did ask her if you'd heard, and she said yes, you all had except Lenny.
Lenny What?
Fran She hasn't told him yet apparently. She's very worried about how he'll take it.
Lenny Take what?
Fran The news.
Lenny What news?
Fran About the baby.
Lenny What baby? I don't understand — what do you mean, "baby"?
Fran They're like people only very small.
Lenny Whose baby?
Fran Dee Dee's.
Lenny Dee Dee's having a baby?
Fran Yes.
Lenny Dee Dee's pregnant.
Fran That too.
Lenny Oh — my God.
Fran Are you all right?

Lenny is pole-axed. From the laptop we hear the awful laugh of the monkey again. Lenny walks out of the basement front door in a stupor

Hallo? Hallo? Hallo?

Fran continues to call out "Hallo" as —

— *the* Curtain *falls*

ACT II

The same

When the CURTAIN *rises the living-room is lit. Candles are burning and the remains of a Moroccan dinner — plates, dishes, empty wine glasses — are on the floor, perhaps on a tray. Gus, wearing a colourful Moroccan robe, sits on the floor; Letitia is behind him with her hands on his head. Her eyes are closed and she seems to be in a trance*

Letitia Miranda ... Miranda ... Are you there?
Gus You're not getting anything? She's not there?
Letitia Some spirits can be quite bashful.
Gus Not Miranda, she wasn't bashful, she was a karaoke champion.
Letitia Ssssh. I am trying to commune with your psyche. (*Indicating his head*) I'm having trouble getting through. There's a lot going on up there.
Gus Well, we're right bang on the flight path into Heathrow.
Letitia Tut, tut. Don't be a silly cynical Gus ... (*Putting her hands on his head*) There is much confusion in here. Confusion and stress.
Gus Ah, that's probably because I'm confused and stressed.
Letitia You're worried about Lenny? Is that it?
Gus He does this when he can't cope. He goes walkabout, just takes to the hills. Three days he's been gone with nothing but his walking boots. He's got a lot on his plate.
Letitia (*fishing*) You mean — with the baby?
Gus I didn't know you knew.
Letitia I didn't, but I do now. Where is Dee Dee by the way?
Gus She's gone late-night shopping with her mother.
Letitia How far gone is she?
Gus The King's Road, I think.
Letitia (*smacking his head*) The baby, you naughty man.
Gus About ten weeks.
Letitia (*in tune with the spirits*) A little boy if I read things aright.
Gus She'll be safe buying pink then. Poor old Lenny, a grandfather — he'll be in quite a state.
Letitia Myrtle will soon sort him out when she gets here.
Gus What?
Letitia She'll be home soon.
Gus What? ... I mean how? What have you done?

Act II

Letitia I brought a little teensy weeny bit of pressure to bear. I told her publishers I'd call the *News of the World*. I said I needed sight of Myrtle in the flesh, live and kicking on my show or she'd fetch up with a nasty old dose of the tabloids. She'll be on the show, you can bet your sweet life.
Gus The two of them together, Lenny and Myrtle live, on your show — I *must* remember to set the video. Letish, I thought we had an agreement that she didn't have to.
Letitia I know. Aren't I a mischievous little kitten? Now come here. Sit. Where were we?
Gus Looking for Miranda.

Letitia puts her hands on Gus's head again. She peers at his scalp

Letitia There's a special shampoo you can get for that. (*In her trance again*) Miranda. Yes ... How many wives have you had, Gus?
Gus Just the four — but it's Miranda I'm after.
Letitia What about the others? Have they yet surrendered their corporeal personas?
Gus What?
Letitia Handed in their dinner plates. You don't want to commune with them — they're not dead?
Gus No, I've got them all on Direct Debit.
Letitia So Miranda was the last actual incumbent?
Gus Yup — she died in office.
Letitia (*resuming her communing*) Miranda ... She's dark?
Gus No.
Letitia Tall?
Gus No.
Letitia Thin?
Gus No.
Letitia Yes, yes ... I'm getting a short chunky blonde ...
Gus Astounding ...
Letitia It's a gift.
Gus Is she there?
Letitia She's there ... She's coming among us ...
Gus She's not among me is she? Hallo pet. Everything OK? How does she seem?
Letitia A bit tetchy actually. She says — "What do you want?"
Gus (*to the spirit, confidentially*) The thing is, pet, I've forgotten our PIN code at the Woolwich.
Letitia She says she cleaned you out before she popped her clogs. (*Archly*) She's jealous. She thinks there's someone new you fancy.
Gus No, no. In the real world all I've got is my curry fantasy. (*In heaven*) Vindaloo followed by Edwina.

Letitia (*laughing at Miranda's joke*) No indeed.
Gus What?
Letitia She says you've still got the same crass sense of humour. (*Heeding Miranda. Delightedly*) What? ... Do you? ... Do you really?
Gus What she saying?
Letitia (*modestly*) She says she thinks you and I'd make a lovely couple ... Oh, she's beginning to fade.
Gus See if you can get her on VHF.
Letitia No — she gone. So, what about us, Gus?
Gus Us, Gus?
Letitia Are you in a meaningful relationship?
Gus Relationship — yes. Meaningful — no.
Letitia How long has it been going on?
Gus Since — last Thursday tea-time. She runs the Pilates class at the day centre.
Letitia And the long term prospects are ... ?
Gus Short. Her husband is coming out of hospital next week.
Letitia (*lustily*) You are a truly rotten bastard, aren't you?
Gus (*nearly kissing her*) I do my best.

The upper front door opens and Dee Dee and Fran enter with shopping bags etc.

(*Seeing Dee Dee*) Ah, the cavalry ... .
Dee Dee Hi, Grampi. Hallo, Letitia.
Letitia Dee Dee, my dear girl, how are you? Hallo, Fran.
Fran Hallo, nice to see you again. I don't know which is the more exhausted — my feet or my Visa card.
Dee Dee Still no sign of Dad, Grampi? He hasn't rung?
Gus No, my darling. He'll be back soon I expect for a change of sock.
Fran He's probably just having a good old think.
Gus A good old think is three minutes not three days. Unless he's on "auto repeat".
Letitia He's probably trying to come terms with the situation in which he is.
Dee Dee You mean the spout up which I am.
Gus But who told him? That's what I can't work out.
Fran About the baby? Myrtle, I suppose.
Gus ⎫
Dee Dee ⎬ (*together*) Myrtle?
Gus Myrtle told Lenny about Dee Dee's baby? I think I'm losing the plot.
Dee Dee So who told her, then?
Fran I did. On the phone. You said everybody knew except your dad.
Dee Dee Ah. That would be it then. Myrtle told Dad.

Act II

Fran I expect she did it very tactfully.
Gus I bet she did.
Dee Dee Poor old Dad. He's painted himself into a bit of a corner.
Fran You don't think he's gone on a binge?
Dee Dee He's not good at that; his idea of a binge is half a shandy and a packet of Wotsits.
Fran (*to Dee Dee*) Well, I think I win my bet.
Gus What bet is that?
Fran That you two would meet up again. Do I detect a certain frisson in the air?
Gus Oh dear. It's probably my high fibre diet.
Dee Dee (*reminding Gus of his fine for bad jokes*) That'll be one pound at least, Grampi. (*Explaining to Letitia*) He has to pay for his jokes.
Letitia I wish I'd known; I could have made a fortune.
Fran (*sniffing*) You haven't been cooking, have you, Gus?
Letitia He made me a lovely (*her face registers "it wasn't at all"*) — what was it exactly?
Gus Couscous à la sultana.
Letitia (*dubiously*) So it was. Delicious.
Fran (*to Letitia*) I've got some Imodium in my bag when you need it.
Dee Dee We've been out on a mega shop — wedding dress for Mum and maternity for me.
Gus Actually, I got you a present, myself. (*He produces an Arsenal "babygro" in a bag and gives it to Dee Dee*)
Dee Dee Oh, Grampi — that is adorable.
Gus I thought it might help me with the bonding.
Dee Dee What if it's a girl?
Gus I'll take it back. I've still got the receipt.
Dee Dee (*to Fran*) Come on, Mum, let's put this lot in my room.
Fran (*to Letitia*) You want to watch out Letitia — he's a bit of a H.O.G.A.C.T. (*Explaining*) Horny Old Goat After Closing Time.

Dee Dee exits followed by Fran

Letitia So you're into fantasizing are you, Gus?
Gus Well, we all need a bit of a kick start from time to time.
Letitia Do you know what mine is, Gus? My fantasy.
Gus I shudder to think.

Letitia whispers in his ear. Gus likes what he hears. He giggles and then checks himself

Gus I'm afraid bondage is not really my cup of tea. I had a rather scary experience in a club down the Old Kent Road last Bank Holiday.

Letitia Then how about a winter cruise round the Seychelles. Just you and me?
Gus But the last game at Highbury isn't until May.
Letitia Oh, I could show you a game of two halves, big boy.

Lenny, as Myrtle, enters like a whirlwind through the front door

Lenny Peek-a-boo everybody. Auntie's home. Letitia ... .
Letitia (*going to Lenny; thrilled*) Myrtle! Myrtle. I knew you'd come.
Gus Gordon Bennett ... (*Taking in Myrtle's costume*) The Return of The Jedi.
Letitia At last we meet.
Lenny We do. We do indeed. Letitia. How do you do?
Letitia There you are, Myrtle, in the flesh.
Lenny And there you are. Both of us in the flesh.
Letitia Such style — style and beauty.
Lenny (*taking in Gus's robe*) Give over. What have we got here? "Mr Blobby Goes to Marrakesh". Or are you disguised as a deck chair? My feet are killing me — I've been traipsing up and down Oxford Street.
Gus You're lucky not to have been arrested.
Letitia Now you two are not to be all "Snooty the Snoot" with one another. Gus, give Myrtle a nice welcome home kiss.
Gus (*horrified*) No.
Letitia No? What do you mean, no?
Gus I mean no. No kiss. No thank you. No way.
Letitia Gus, don't be a horrid Mr Grumpy — give her a kiss.
Gus I can't. I won't.
Lenny Oh, Gussie-kins, give Myrtle a nice kissy-wissy. (*Puckering up*) Force yourself.

Gus is revolted by the idea and very reluctant, but at last kisses Lenny with a bad grace

Aren't you pleased to see me, Gus?
Gus I wasn't expecting you.
Lenny I wasn't expecting me either, but pressure has been brought to bear, *n'est-ce-pas*, Letitia?
Letitia I've been a mischievous little bunny, haven't I, Myrtle?
Lenny You have blackmailed me into coming all this way just to show you that I am in sound working order.
Gus She was worried that Lenny had been invading your aura.
Lenny He hasn't been anywhere near it. Bless him. So now you can tell all your viewers that I'm the real McCoy.
Letitia Oh yes, indeed. I can spot a fake like that ... (*She tries but fails to click her fingers*)

Act II

Gus Letitia is nobody's fool. She is very keen to get some footage of you on her programme, Myrtle — isn't that nice?
Letitia "Mind Your Own Business" needs you, Myrtle.
Lenny We'll have to see what Lenny has to say about that, won't we? (*Sniffing the air*) Gus, you haven't been cooking have you?
Letitia Yes — a lovely ——
Gus — couscous à la sultana.
Lenny (*to Letitia*) I've got some Imodium in my bag when you need it.
Letitia Oh Myrtle, I am so thrilled to meet you.
Lenny I am a big girl, aren't I? Much taller than I expected.
Letitia I've always felt that you and I were two of a kind.
Gus I wouldn't put your last half crown on it.
Letitia (*forcefully*) I don't like any jiggery-pokery.
Lenny Me neither — especially not the pokery.

Dee Dee enters. She is stupefied by seeing Myrtle

Dee Dee (*after a pause*) Dad ——

Lenny lets out a stifled howl

(*Whoops!*) — is still not home then.
Lenny It's me darling, your aunt Myrtle.
Dee Dee What a surprise.
Lenny Yes, isn't it? But this naughty little bunny gave me no choice. So here I am. Let me give you a nice kiss. (*He kisses Dee Dee*)
Dee Dee It's very good to see you. Very good indeed.
Lenny Also I wanted to tell you how thrilled I am about your news. You'll make a wonderful mother.

They embrace. Lenny takes a moment with his daughter

Dee Dee Er ... You know that Dad's gone walkabout.
Lenny He's such a silly billy, but I've had a long chat with him. We had lunch together at the Savoy.
Gus Him in his hiking boots and you in Cherie Blair's cast-offs? I wish I'd been there.
Lenny He asked me to tell you that he's very proud and happy. And he can't wait to be a grandfather.
Letitia If you ask me he's a daft old dinosaur with his head up his arse.
Lenny That's a visual image I shall long cherish, Letish. (*To Dee Dee*) Your Dad's not always been very good at expressing himself. I think he feels he's failed you, my darling, by not being the kind of father you could talk to and confide in.

Dee Dee That's why you're here, right?
Lenny He wanted me to talk to you. (*Heartfelt*) I think he's just a little sad that he was the last member of the family to be told. He should have been the first.
Dee Dee Well, a close second perhaps.
Lenny The trouble is he probably still sees you as gummy little girl with freckles and pigtails.
Dee Dee He's a wonderful dad.
Lenny Is he?
Dee Dee Mm. He always said there was nothing that I couldn't tell him, nothing he wouldn't understand.
Lenny Apart from the plot of *Pulp Fiction*, you mean.
Gus (*chuckling*) Do you remember telling her the facts of life?
Lenny Yes ... (*Whoops!*) No, but I'm sure her father does.
Dee Dee He was always so good at explaining things to me.
Gus Cricket and evolution and how to make cakes, maybe.
Dee Dee He always stammers really badly talking about sex and things.
Letitia Don't tell me he had to sing the facts of life to you?
Dee Dee It was before he started the Cantartherapy. He did a demonstration, bless him, with a bread stick and a canneloni.
Gus *The Joy of Sex* is alive and well at Pizza Hut.
Dee Dee (*as Lenny*) "You see, my darling — making love is a bit like d-d-dancing — only lying down."
Letitia Aaaaah. The dear boy.
Dee Dee Then we got terrible giggles when the bread stick snapped.
Gus I know the feeling.
Dee Dee He said sex only worked with someone you were in love with.
Gus Will he never learn?
Dee Dee *And* it had to be in the dark.
Lenny (*agreeing*) Oh yes, certainly, lights off.
Gus I must give that a try.
Letitia Would that be such a novelty for you, Gus?
Gus I'm an everything-on man myself.
Letitia Everything on?
Gus The lights, the telly, the socks.
Letitia There's something to be said for having the lights off at our age, isn't there, Myrtle?
Lenny Definitely. And a general anaesthetic too in my case.
Gus I've always seen sex as being a bit like Happy Hour.
Letitia A thing of joy?
Gus No. You have to get as much of it as you can before the price goes up.
Lenny You sweet old-fashioned thing, Gus. You know he once told me that Lenny was conceived while he was watching *Match of The Day*. Isn't that right?

Act II

Gus Yes indeed. Arsenal were in the FA Cup quarter final.
Letitia Very romantic.
Gus (*proudly*) Oh yes. Two all ... It went to extra time.
Lenny Don't tell me, there was a penalty shoot out. (*He smirks and then checks himself*)
Dee Dee Yuk ... Too much information. Here. (*She gives Lenny a photograph from her bag or pocket*)
Lenny What's this?
Dee Dee It's my baby. A photograph of the scan.
Lenny The baby in — in ... (*Pointing to Dee Dee's tummy*) In there.
Dee Dee Yes.
Lenny (*studying the photograph*) Looks like something trapped in a tumble drier. Is that the right way up?
Dee Dee Yes.
Lenny Very avant garde in black and white.
Gus (*peering at the photograph*) It's a boy.
Dee Dee No.
Gus (*pointing*) What's that then — a chipolata?
Dee Dee That's the umbilical cord, Grampi. They don't know yet.
Gus Look at that, will you. (*Very moved*) I've never seen an Arsenal supporter that small.

Fran enters in her wedding outfit. She does not immediately see Myrtle

Fran (*with a flourish*) There we are — a sneak preview. What do you think?
Dee Dee It's lovely Mum. Terrific ... (*Things are tricky here*) I don't think you ever met Dad's aunt. This is my mother Francis Loftus. Myrtle Banbury.

Lenny passes out. Gus catches him and hoists him up with his hands on "Myrtle's" breasts. Lenny realizes and moves Gus's hands

Fran I am so pleased to meet you. I thought you were up the Amazon.
Lenny (*pole-axed*) I think I probably am. I didn't know you were here.
Fran Of course I feel as if I've known you for years.
Lenny And me you.
Fran I'm such a big fan of yours. It's quite unmistakable.
Lenny What is?
Fran (*studying his/her face*) The family resemblance. Lenny's got your cheekbones.
Gus He's got a little something of his father's too.
Fran Well, this is quite a party, isn't it?
Gus (*ominously*) Oh yes. It could turn out to be a surprise party.
Letitia Oh, good. What's the surprise?

Gus You wouldn't believe it if I told you.
Fran (*showing off her dress*) What do you think?
Letitia Gorgeous. You look quite lovely, my dear. Doesn't she Myrtle?
Lenny Yes ... She does, quite lovely ...
Dee Dee Mum, Auntie Myrtle has had lunch with Dad and it's all sorted, isn't that right?
Lenny Yes. We had a little chat.
Fran You straightened him out. You are so clever.
Lenny If you ask me Lenny's just a daft old dinosaur with his head up his arse.
Gus What you might call a head-up-his-arse-asaurus.
Fran Actually with Lenny being Lenny I can't think how you found the opportunity to get pregnant in the first place. (*She laughs*)
Lenny (*laughing too, but curious*) Yes, quite. I mean how did you manage it — with Lenny being Lenny?
Gus Piece of cake. She told him she was going on a bell-ringing weekend at Wells Cathedral.
Lenny The little minx. And where was she in reality?
Gus Shacked up with Justin in a tent at the Glastonbury Festival.
Lenny Glastonbury? All that mud. Promise me you won't call the baby Moonbeam or Trixiebell.
Dee Dee I promise.
Gus Just be grateful it's not called Mondeo.
Lenny Mondeo? Is that a Latin American name? When's it due?
Dee Dee April seventeenth.
Letitia And will Daddy be there with you for the birth?
Lenny Certainly not.
Letitia I meant the baby's daddy.
Dee Dee I'm afraid not; he's otherwise engaged.
Letitia You don't think he should be there for the birth?
Gus He only just made it for the conception.
Lenny What are you saying, my darling?
Dee Dee I'm going solo. I can manage without him.
Lenny Oh no, my darling, it's a job for two, believe me. Being a single parent is like riding tandem with nobody at the handlebars.
Dee Dee Look, I'm not going to get all Doris Day about it.
Lenny What do you mean?
Gus Her Rock Hudson's done a runner.
Lenny I don't understand. Surely Justin is ...
Dee Dee With Mandy.
Lenny Mandy? Who's she? Who's Mandy?
Gus She's a junior stylist at Toni and Guy. All frizzy hair and too posh to wash.

Act II

Lenny Oh my God.
Letitia Your father won't be very happy about that, will he?
Lenny No he will not. A junior stylist.
Fran Poor Lenny was always a bit of a stickler. He wanted us to wait till after the wedding before we went all the way. You know before he'd go the whole hog. (*To Dee Dee*) I never dared tell him we'd had a glitch.
Dee Dee A glitch?
Lenny (*discombobulated*) A glitch?
Fran Well, he thinks to this day that you were born two months premature.
Lenny Premature? You mean she wasn't?
Fran Not at nine pounds thirteen ounces, thank you very much ... Luckily he never gave it a moment's thought.
Lenny You mean Dee Dee was in fact conceived on the wrong side of the duvet?
Fran Yes.
Lenny Are you sure?
Fran Yes ...
Lenny You'd think Lenny would have noticed. He's got such a good head for figures.
Fran You're not shocked, are you?
Lenny Good lord no, I just don't understand quite how ... ?
Gus Well, you know sometimes you see tufts of grass growing way up in the chimney of an old building and you think "How in hell did the seed get up there?" It's a bit like that.
Lenny Dee Dee was not conceived on a gust of wind, Gus.
Fran It was in Broadstairs, actually.
Lenny (*involuntarily*) At the Holiday Inn.
All (*variously*) What? Eh? (*etc.*)
Lenny Oh the holiday *in* Broadstairs — that you probably had.
Fran He was at a conference. I missed the last train home. We'd had a Chinese take-away in his room and a bottle of rather sweet wine. And we shared this packet of Liquorice Allsorts. (*Laughing*) Goodness me, we laughed.
Lenny Oh yes — I mean I bet you did.
Fran He said he'd sleep on the floor, bless him.
Lenny He's always been a very honourable man.
Fran (*with a dirty laugh*) Not for long he wasn't. There was a terrible draught down there.
Letitia You mean he climbed up into the bed?
Fran No. I joined him down on the floor.
Gus Yuk ... Too much information.
Lenny But surely then you were both in the draught.
Fran Exactly. That was always your father's trouble.

Lenny What? Oh do tell.
Fran He was always just so shy — so *undemonstrative*.
Letitia That's what we girls like, a proper outright declaration.
Fran We want to be overwhelmed. We want our knight in shining armour to defy danger and sweep us off our feet.
Lenny So it's no good Lenny faffing about then. He's got to do something bold, has he?
Fran Absolutely.
Letitia Oh Myrtle, Lenny could have learnt so much from you. All those little feminine secrets that men need to know.
Fran Is it all right if I just pop down to the study and make a quick call to Luigi?
Dee Dee Sure.

Fran exits from the living-room

Lenny Why don't you two take Letitia to find a taxi?
Gus I could give you a lift on my Vespa.

Dee Dee exits through the upper front door

Gus follows Dee Dee. Letitia hangs back

Letitia (*coyly; to Gus*) Lead on, Mr Blobby.

Gus exits

The Lights come up in the study

Fran enters the study and dials a telephone number

So, Myrtle, we'll do a wee bit of filming for "Mind Your Own Business". OK?
Lenny I'll talk to Lenny. It's his call.
Letitia Oh, super. Cue the lights. Cue the music. Action! Oh, Myrtle ... You'll be sensational.
Lenny It's been great meeting you.
Letitia (*gripping Myrtle*) Take care, my dear, I'm getting turquoise. All around you.
Lenny Oh dear, it's not really me. Are you sure?
Letitia Oh yes. Turquoise tells its own sorry story.

Letitia exits

Act II

Lenny (*closing the door*) Bog off — you nosey old cow. (*He picks up the telephone and eavesdrops*)
Fran (*into the study telephone, sexily*) No you can't see it, not until the wedding, Luigi *caro* ... Will you? Under the mosquito net ... ?

It's too much for Lenny. He makes the sound of terrible static down the telephone and then unplugs it so that Fran's line goes dead

Lenny exits down the stairs

The living-room lights fade to black-out

Fran (*into the telephone*) Hallo ... hallo ... Luigi ... *pronto* ... (*She re-dials*)

Lenny enters the study

Lenny Everything all right?
Fran We got cut off.
Lenny Oh I am sorry. Oh, dear, poor old Giuseppi?
Fran Luigi.
Lenny Whatever. All set for the big day in Bermuda?
Fran Barbados. Yes. It's all looking pretty good. Pity none of you can come.
Lenny Not really. In-laws are one thing, out-laws quite another. It's a beautiful dress. It was pale blue last time, wasn't it? (*He pours them both a glass of wine*)
Fran Yes — and a silly little hat.
Lenny With a bow on it ... I saw the photographs. So you think you've got it right this time?
Fran Yeah. No hat. Lime green. Yes, Luigi loves me.
Lenny So did Lenny, surely.
Fran Yeah. In his way. It's a funny old business, love, isn't it?
Lenny A bit like athlete's foot, I always think. (*He hands Fran a glass*)
Fran In what way?
Lenny Just when you think you've got over it, up it comes and hits you — smack between the toes. Cheers.
Fran To the future.
Lenny Whatever that is. Cheers.
Fran I wish I'd met you before — perhaps you could have helped us, Lenny and me.
Lenny Oh, I don't know about that.
Fran We were so young and naïve when we got married ... What did we know?
Lenny He knew nothing. Of course, as his aunt I had done my best to teach him about things. Those little feminine secrets that men need to know about.

Fran Such as?
Lenny (*completely stumped*) I've forgotten.
Fran You should have told him not to be so bleeding nice all the time. He nearly drove me mad with his oh-so-perfect manners.
Lenny Opening doors and things you mean?
Fran More in the bedroom really. When it comes down to it, we don't want "motor-mouth", do we? We want Action Man.
Lenny Oh, I see. A bit of a chatterbox was he?
Fran Yeah ... I mean you know how it is for us girls.
Lenny No ... Yes ... Remind me.
Fran We don't want interruption when we're trying to fantasize. How can a girl concentrate on George Clooney with her husband wittering away under the duvet? "Did you put the cat out? Shall I do the school run? I think I've got my pyjama cord knotted ... How was it for you, dear? Was it all right for you? Shall I get you a nice cup of Horlicks?" Didn't anyone ever tell him that we don't want that sort of stuff? There are times when girls don't want to chat.
Lenny Don't be ridiculous. That can't be true, surely.
Fran That's what I get from Luigi, you see.
Lenny What?
Fran Big, silent, macho vibes.
Lenny I'm so glad. But no Horlicks?
Fran He's rugged — ruthless. Completely overpowering ... .
Lenny A sort of an Italian Rupert Murdoch, you mean? I think I need another drink.
Fran Lenny was just too damn nice all the time.
Lenny Oh, yes, he's always been the kind of wimp who'd give up his seat to a pregnant woman on a crowded bus.
Fran I just have this weakness for complete bastards. Is that perverse, do you think?
Lenny Oh, no, my dear, nothing is perverse these days, what with cloned sheep and gay bishops. Bastards are all very well on the side, you know, for recreational purposes, for a dirty weekend or a wet afternoon but in the real world — you're better off with the Horlicks.
Fran No George Clooney then?
Lenny Not as a main course. If a man doesn't remember your birthday or know your dress size, what's the point?
Fran You are fabulous. So wise.
Lenny Aren't I just?
Fran It's a pity you never had children. You'd have made a marvellous mother.
Lenny I don't think I was quite cut out for it.
Fran (*taking a manuscript out of her bag*) I read your manuscript by the way.

Act II 45

I absolutely loved it but you know the bit at the end where Ingrid meets Joshua in the Lake District — the big reunion ... ?
Lenny Oh yes. The last chapter.
Fran (*turning the pages*) There's a blistering storm and the rain is pelting down, and they haven't seen each other for six years and they take shelter in a sort of cave, half-way up the mountain and they share a picnic all alone. It's the perfect setting and what does he bloody well talk about? The ozone layer.
Lenny Yes, well it is a problem. All those emissions.
Fran Are you serious?
Lenny I am indeed. (*Gazing at her*) It's caused by all our old fridges apparently.
Fran We want him to say what he's really feeling as he gazes into her eyes. He has to *tell* her.
Lenny You mean while she's eating his (*mispronouncing it "cibatta"*) ciabatta?
Fran (*saying it correctly*) Ciabatta.
Lenny Whatever. You don't think it's implicit?
Fran Implicit is not good enough. A woman wants it spelt out.
Lenny C.I.A.B.A.T.T.A.
Fran I'm still crazy about you.
Lenny (*entranced*) I beg your pardon.
Fran That's what she wants to hear.
Lenny I see, you mean, kind of how he's still utterly crazily in love with you — *her*, after all these years, how he's never loved anyone else. Never could.
Fran Exactly. She wants all the details of how and why he loves her. Every minute detail ...
Lenny You mean things like — the blueness of her eyes and the sound of her laughter, and the smoothness of her skin and the backs of her knees when she's going upstairs in front of me. *Him.*
Fran Yes, yes, that sort of thing.
Lenny And the way she has of whispering ...
Fran Go on.
Lenny Exactly, when we're making love.
Fran What?
Lenny (*correcting himself*) They. Them. Making love ...
Fran Exactly. We want to know what it feels like being a man in that situation?
Lenny (*crossing his legs*) Not very comfortable, I should think.

Things are awkward between them

Fran Can I ask you something?
Lenny What?

Fran Are you at all ... ?
Lenny What?
Fran Bi ...
Lenny Bye. You're not leaving?
Fran No not bye. Bi.
Lenny Not bye-bye ... Not bye as in bye-bye ... (*Realizing*) You mean bi as in bisec ... bisec ... gay?
Fran Yeah. Have you ever thought about sex with a woman?
Lenny Yes. No. (*Horrified*) You mean as a woman? With a woman?
Fran Yes. You're a woman.
Lenny Yes, I am. I'm a woman ... I have always been a one-woman man. (*Whoops*) A one-man woman. A one on one — sort of person. I don't think I'd be any good at it.
Fran What?
Lenny Being gay. I wouldn't know who needs what doing to whom with what. I know nothing, a complete ignoramus. I even used to think a vibrator was one of those things they use to dig up roads.
Fran That's a compressor.
Lenny No wonder I wasn't having much fun.
Fran That's the problem isn't it — the old G spot.
Lenny Oh yes. I can't bear cheap furniture.
Fran G spot — not G Plan.
Lenny (*laughing it off*) Of course, silly me, what would a lesbian want with a cheap coffee table?
Fran I suppose at least it might be easier to find. (*She laughs*)

Lenny joins in the laughter and is then nonplussed

Lenny So you think Joshua has got to make his move. A bold move.
Fran Yes — then the story can have a happy ending, can't it?
Lenny Are happy endings what we really want? Don't they just fill us with impossible dreams? In fiction kissing in the rain and making love on the beach are all very well but in the real world you just end up with pneumonia and cystitis. In the real world people don't call you tomorrow.

Fran fetches her mobile from her bag. She dials a number during the following

What are you doing?
Fran Calling him.
Lenny Who?
Fran (*dialling*) Lenny, on his mobile. I want to talk to him.
Lenny Stop. Don't do it. He won't like it.

Act II

Fran To hell with that. (*She makes to hit the last digit*)
Lenny Perhaps he's busy — or asleep — or half-way up a mountain.
Fran At any rate, he has to ask himself certain questions.
Lenny Such as?
Fran Where is he heading? And what does he want in life? How's that for starters?
Lenny Right up there with prawn cocktail and Caesar Salad.
Fran He needs to ask himself who the hell he is underneath it all.
Lenny (*alarmed*) Don't even begin to go there.
Fran What's he going to do about Dee Dee? About Gus? About the baby? About you?
Lenny Me? He'll probably kill me.
Fran And what does he feel about *me*?
Lenny You?
Fran What does he feel about me, Myrtle? (*Pressing the last digit*) Hm? He needs to get that quite clear.

The mobile starts to ring loudly in "Myrtle's" handbag. Lenny picks up the bag and slams it down forcefully on the desk. The ringing stops, but after a beat the phone rings again, this time in a damaged tone. Lenny takes off his shoe and hits the bag several times to kill the sound, the ring-tone changing to an injured sound as he hits the bag again and again. The ring-tone then signals a painful death followed by the flat-line sound of a hospital heart monitor

Lenny Dratted things. Why do we never listen when they tell us to switch them off. (*He takes out the very battered, completely smashed mobile*)
Fran "The future is not so Orange." All I'm saying is he has to stop burying his head in the sand.
Lenny He will, in his own time. (*Opening the door*) What's it to you if he is anyway?
Fran What?
Lenny Not quite clear about what he feels about you. It's none of your business. Goodbye.

Fran hits the redial button and a feeble ringing tone comes from the mobile in Lenny's hand

You deal with it. (*He drops the telephone into the goldfish tank*)

Immediately the water in the goldfish tank bubbles frantically. The goldfish tank lights, and those of the living-room, flicker

Fran exits

Lenny takes off his wig. He is snookered. Morosely he sits and takes a tea-cake out from each side of his bra. He broods and then eventually eats one of the tea-cakes

Fran enters. She is amazed and appalled at what she sees

Lenny freezes, holding a tea-cake in each hand

Lenny (*his mouth full*) I know what you're going to say.
Fran No, you don't. You do not know what I'm going to say because I don't know what I'm going to say. What do you think I'm going to say?
Lenny You're going to say: what sort of fool do you take me for, you bastard?
Fran That'll do. (*Referring to the teacakes*) Nice tits.
Lenny Thanks.
Fran Am I the last one to know?
Lenny No, after Dee Dee and Gus, you're the third, but I think the cashier at Debenhams is beginning to smell a rat. Are you going to hit me?
Fran It's an option. How dare you be so much less boring than I thought you were. What about you? What are you going to say?
Lenny Please. Please don't tell Letitia.
Fran Why kill the golden goose? Is that all?
Lenny I've got a selection of Jaeger frocks ——

Fran looks at him

(*Seeing the look*) — that I don't suppose you want to borrow.
Fran I'll tell you the thing I've never understood about cross-dressing: where do you put it?
Lenny What?
Fran You know — your meat and two veg.
Lenny Well, I've always been a tidy packer.
Fran (*moving to exit and standing in the doorway*) And to think I nearly asked you to be my bridesmaid.

Fran exits to the street

The Lights go down on the study

Lenny exits to the kitchen

The Lights come up on the living-room

Dee Dee and Gus enter. Gus sits at the laptop

Act II 49

Dee Dee Now Grampi, have you got all the cue cards sorted?
Gus It'll never work. Your father's gone mad.
Dee Dee It's always a worry when he says he has a plan.
Gus Like Baldric only worse. We can't fake a telephone conference call on national television.
Dee Dee Yes, we can ... We have the technology. Here ...

Dee Dee presses a key on the laptop

Lenny (*as Myrtle; voice-over*) Hallo there Letitia, my dear, I'm so sorry I can't be with you in person on "Mind Your Own Business", as I promised. I suddenly had to get back to Brazil, to my little adobe haçienda. Please forgive me.
Gus We will never get away with it.
Dee Dee We have to. We could be ruined — exposed.
Gus She'll suss it. Letitia is not stupid.
Dee Dee I don't know about that. (*Pressing another key*) What do you think Myrtle? Is Letitia a stupid old cow?
Lenny (*as Myrtle; voice-over*) Oh yes, in my opinion most certainly.
Gus We are going to be doing this in front of 11 million people.

Dee Dee presses another key

Lenny (*as Myrtle; voice-over*) I tell you it'll be a piece of cake.

The telephone rings. Gus answers it.

Gus (*into the phone*) Hallo. Gus Loftus Enterprises. ... Yes, it is. ... Oh. ... Hi, there dude, are you hangin' loose? ... I'm hangin' *very* loose too. (*Offering the phone to Dee Dee*) It's Justin.
Dee Dee (*not taking it*) I'm not speaking to him.
Gus (*into the phone*) She's not speaking to you. (*To Dee Dee*) Why not?
Dee Dee I hate him.
Gus (*into the phone*) She hates you. (*To Dee Dee*) He says: "Come on, tush, don't give us a 'ard time." (*He listens to Justin*) Have you? (*To Dee Dee*) He's given Mandy the elbow. Frizzy and too posh to wash — gone.
Dee Dee He's got rid of her?
Gus (*into the phone*) Here. Tell her yourself. (*To Dee Dee*) Dee Dee ... (*Into the phone*) Hang on, Justin ... Dee Dee. (*He offers the telephone to Dee Dee*)

Dee Dee won't take the phone from Gus. He follows her round the room with the telephone during the following

(*Into the phone*) She's not talking to you. (*To Dee Dee*) Please. (*Into the phone*) She's shaking her head. (*To Dee Dee*) Please.

Dee Dee gives Justin the finger

(*Into the phone*) She's giving you the finger. ... Can you hear that? I did ask nicely. ... What? ... Oh my God ... OK. (*He goes down on one knee, with difficulty. He takes the following lines from Justin. To Dee Dee*) He wants you back. Please. He wants you to move in with him.

Dee Dee Has he gone bonkers?

Gus (*into the phone*) Have you gone bonkers? ... (*To Dee Dee*) He's got a new pad. Really cool. Right next to a Burger King. It's got a bathroom and all.

Dee Dee What's all this about?

Gus (*into the telephone*) Justin, what's all this about? ... (*To Dee Dee*) He's says he's cleaning up his act, man. (*Into the telephone*) ... Have you? ... Have you? ... Have you? ... .

Dee Dee What's he saying?

Gus He's had his dreadlocks off, his nose ring off and his tattoos removed.

Dee Dee Hang up, Grampi. Hang up.

Gus No, I want to hear what else he's had amputated.

Dee Dee (*heading for the exit*) Tell him to bog off, the great weasly plonker.

Dee Dee exits

Gus (*into the phone*) I think she needs time to think it over, Justin. She doesn't understand why you've changed your tune. You don't want your kid to be a little — yes, well these days we only use that word for referees. ... Yeah, you hang loose. Bye. (*He hangs up*)

The Lights come up on the study

Dee Dee enters the study, on her mobile to Fran

Dee Dee (*into the mobile*) Can't wait. ... Good luck. Love you too. ... Bye.

Lenny enters anxiously with his cue cards

Dee Dee hangs up

Lenny Was that Justin, by any chance?

Dee Dee No, it was not. It was Mum actually. She's on her way to the airport.

During the following Dee Dee puts chairs in place for the interview. She takes a tiny loudspeaker from the desk drawer and puts it under the desk to relay "Myrtle's" voice

Lenny Oh I see. You don't think we should have one last rehearsal with the actual telephone? I'm a bit nervous. (*To the camera*) Is Dad upstairs? (*Into the intercom*) Hallo ... .

Dee Dee puts the telephone on the table for the interview

Gus (*into the intercom*) Hallo there.
Lenny (*into the intercom*) How do I look?
Gus (*into the intercom*) Like someone auditioning for a Prozac commercial.
Dee Dee (*into the intercom*) Dad wants another rehearsal.
Gus (*into the intercom*) OK, but the show is going to start any minute. Letitia's in the make-up van. Raring to go.
Dee Dee Here we are, Dad, put your earpiece in.

Lenny puts in his wee earpiece

Lenny (*to the camera*) Testing, testing.
Dee Dee (*into the intercom*) Use the mike, Grampi ...
Lenny Say something.

Gus picks up the microphone and speaks into Lenny's ear

Gus (*into the microphone*) This is never going to work.
Lenny Say something else.
Gus (*into the microphone*) Give us a smile ...

Lenny smiles

On second thoughts — don't bother.
Dee Dee (*into the intercom*) Cue the telephone. (*She points to a chair*) Dad, there. (*She points to another chair*) Letitia here.
Gus (*into the microphone*) Stand by. Here we go then. (*He presses a key on the laptop*)

The telephone rings in the study

Bingo. On you go ...

Lenny presses a button on the telephone so that they are now in a fake *conference call*

Lenny (*reading from his cards*) Hallo, Myrtle dear, so you've arrived safely back in Brazil, what's the weather like?

Gus presses one of the keys on the laptop

Lenny's voice (*as Myrtle; over the speaker*) Well it's pouring with rain here actually.
Dee Dee Perfect. Try another one — at random.
Lenny (*looking through the cards*) What's your house like? What do you think of women's lib? ... Who do you most admire? No. Here we are. (*Into the telephone*) Myrtle, what foods do you miss most when you're away from England?

Gus is spot on with his cards. He presses a key on the laptop

Lenny's voice (*as Myrtle; over the speaker*) A nice plate of jellied eels and some raspberry jam on toast.

There is a knock at the basement front door

Dee Dee That'll be Letitia. Are you ready?
Lenny Yeah. Please God (*He stays standing, looking flustered*)
Gus (*into the microphone*) The Eagle has landed.
Dee Dee Good luck. (*To Lenny. An order*) Chair. Sit.

Lenny goes to the chair and sits. There's another knock at the basement door

Dee Dee exits up the stairs; she joins Gus in the living-room during the following

Lenny "dries"

Gus (*into the microphone, prompting Lenny*) Say, I wonder who that can be?
Lenny Say, I wonder who that can be? (*Reading his cue card*) "Go and open door" ... Oh yes, of course. (*He moves to the basement front door and opens it*)

Letitia enters

Lenny (*acting, stiffly*) Hallo. Goodness me, it's Letitia Butters. Please do come in.
Letitia Oh, for goodness' sake, that wasn't the real knock on the door.
Lenny (*checking his notes*) Ah. So I don't say that yet?
Letitia No. No this is just me checking you're all set. Is Myrtle standing by to call in?
Lenny Yes. She's raring to go.
Letitia What time is it in Brazil?

Act II   53

Lenny Er ... Late at night.
Gus (*into the microphone*) Early morning.
Lenny (*hearing Gus*) Morning.
Letitia Morning?
Lenny Early morning.
Letitia Good. (*She approaches the camera and addresses it*) Stand by. Ron ... Ron. Is everything OK? (*She looks at Lenny and laughs*) No, I think he always looks like that. (*To Lenny*) I'm on an earpiece.
Lenny You too? (*A gaffe*) You two — can talk to one another. (*He waves to Ron*) Lovely.
Letitia Sometimes we have trouble getting ourselves hooked up, don't we Ron? It was sheer murder with Dale Winton. (*She listens to Ron*) As a row of tents. (*To Ron, then Lenny*) OK my chickabidees, here we go. Let's do it. Take one.

Letitia exits and then pokes her head round the door

Action.

Lenny looks bemused

Think fun, Lenny, think prime-time TV ... Action!

Letitia exits

Lenny moves uneasily to the desk

Dee Dee (*into the microphone*) Relax. Shoulders down. Smile. Sit. *Sit.*

Lenny tries to relax. Then sits. There's a knock at the basement door

Lenny I wonder who that can be? (*He opens the door*)

Letitia enters

Lenny Hello. Goodness me it's Bletitia Tutters. Please do come in.
Letitia Letitia Butters. (*To Ron*) Take two ... Action.

Letitia exits

Lenny starts to relax again. He sits. There is another knock

Lenny I wonder who that can be? (*He opens the door*)

Letitia enters

Lenny Hallo. Goodness me it's Letitia Butters. Please do come in.
Letitia Hallo there. Yes this is Letitia Butters telling you to "Mind Your Own Business".
Lenny (*frozen*) Er ... .
Gus (*into the microphone, prompting*) I'm gobsmacked.
Letitia Me too. (*To the camera*) Yes. This is the home of Myrtle Banbury, that icon of romantic fiction. Sadly she's had to return unexpectedly to Brazil. Viewers, this evening I'm the guest of her nephew, Lenny Loftus.

Lenny is struck dumb

   Aren't I?
Gus (*into the microphone, prompting Lenny*) Yes, that's right; Myrtle Banbury is my aunt.
Lenny Yes, that's right; Myrtle Banbury is my aunt ...
Gus (*into the microphone*) For God's sake, just relax.
Lenny For God's sake, just relax.
Letitia Thank you. Well, it's a lovely room. Very cosy. And this is where the great lady comes when she's in England, is it?
Lenny Yes, indeed.
Letitia You know, viewers, I'm getting the vibes, I'm definitely picking up on Myrtle. This is so much her space. She's here.
Lenny No, no, she's not. She's up the Amazon.
Letitia Her aura is here. I'm getting indigo tinged with a glow of peach. I can definitely feel her.
Lenny Not a good idea, Letitia.
Letitia So, Lenny, you are a statistician, are you?
Lenny Yes. I'm a stat ... stat ... stat ...
Gus (*into the microphone*) — istician.
Lenny Thank you. Yes. I am — one of those.

Lenny refers to his cue cards throughout the following

Letitia And you live here with your daughter, Dee Dee, is that right?
Lenny Yes indeed. She is on her gap year.
Letitia And with your father, Gus, is that right?
Lenny Yes. He's on his sixty-third gap year. You know, I think he'd be great on television himself.
Gus (*into the microphone*) Atta-boy.
Letitia I must say I was so pleased that we are going to be able to link up with your aunt.
Lenny Yes, she has promised to give us a call all the way from Brazil so the three of us can have a little chat.

Act II 55

Letitia It'll be such a thrill to talk to her — the enigmatic Myrtle Banbury.
Lenny Oh yes, there's more to her than meets the eye.
Gus (*into the microphone*) You can say that again.
Lenny (*confused*) Oh yes, there's more to her than meets the eye.
Gus (*into the microphone*) Not you, you prat.
Lenny Not you, you prat.

Dee Dee sets the call in motion

Dee Dee Here we go, Grampi.

The telephone rings in the study

Lenny I expect that will be Myrtle now. (*Answering the telephone*) I'll just press this button here so we can all hear her.
Letitia Good idea.

Lenny presses a telephone button to activate the speaker; this is the "real" conference call

Lenny (*into the phone*) Hallo ... Hallo ... Auntie, is that you? ... Hallo ...

Gus presses a button on the laptop

Lenny's voice (*as Myrtle; over the speaker*) Hallo. Hallo ... Is that you Lenny dear? How nice to hear your voice. Is that gorgeous Letitia Butters there with you?
Lenny (*into the phone*) Yes, Myrtle, you're on "Mind Your Own Business".
Lenny's voice (*as Myrtle; over the speaker*) Oh my goodness! That's my favourite programme. I'm such a big, big fan of Letitia's.
Lenny (*into the phone*) Well she's right here beside me ... Say hallo to her ...

Lenny opens the conference call to Letitia

Letitia (*into the phone*) Hallo, hallo Myrtle. Letitia here ... Hallo.

Nothing. Gus frantically works the controls

Lenny Say hallo, Myrtle?
Gus (*into the microphone*) Hold on ... (*He presses a button*)
Sexy-Voiced Woman (*over the speaker*) Hi there, big boy, my name is Trixie, thank you for calling "Boys Are Us" ...

Letitia reacts. Gus turns the connection off

Gus (*into the microphone*) Oh, bollocks.
Dee Dee What was that, Grampi?
Gus (*to Dee Dee*) An action line — they keep pestering me.
Lenny Hallo ... Hallo ... .
Letitia What was that?
Lenny A crossed line I expect.
Gus Press "Save", Dee Dee. "Save."
Lenny Auntie, can we just ask you a few questions?

Gus flounders with the computer, pressing keys at random

Lenny's voice (*as Myrtle; over the speaker*) Yes. No. Hallo. Goodbye. Brad Pitt. Sleep well. I'm fine.
Lenny (*to Letitia*) Go ahead.
Letitia (*into the phone*) Just to put the rumours to rest, Myrtle, tell us about Lenny. How do you get on with him?
Lenny We get on fine.
Letitia I asked Myrtle.
Lenny We get on fine, don't we?

Gus finds the right key

Lenny's voice (*as Myrtle; over the speaker*) We get on fine.
Lenny We do. We get on fine. Don't we? I love you Auntie.
Lenny's voice (*as Myrtle; over the speaker*) I love you Lenny. I love you Lenny. I love you Lenny ...
Letitia (*to the camera*) There we are, viewers, you've heard it here on "Mind Your Own Business". And what about that rogue, Gus?
Lenny My father? What about him?
Letitia Viewers, I sense I may have awakened in him something that has long been lying dormant.
Gus (*to Dee Dee*) Let sleeping dogs lie, I say.
Letitia I feel it in my waters. Poor baby, he's put me on a pedestal.
Lenny Has he?
Letitia But I just want him to know I could so easily be *knocked off*.
Lenny (*into the phone*) Oh, isn't that a beautiful idea, Myrtle? Wouldn't they make a lovely couple?
Gus Help ... (*He presses a key very firmly*)
Lenny's voice (*as Myrtle; over the speaker*) Sex is terribly over-rated.
Lenny Let's talk about her new book.

Lenny offers Letitia the cue cards with the planned questions. She rejects them

Act II   57

Letitia Yes, yes. (*Into the phone*) Now, Myrtle, tell me, do you reckon that romantic fiction can really survive in the harsh world of today?

Gus presses a button uncertainly

Lenny's voice (*as Myrtle; over the speaker*) Well it's absolutely pouring with rain here actually.
Letitia Pouring with rain ... (*To Lenny, wisely*) A metaphor, I expect. She is remarkable. (*Into the phone again*) So, you don't feel at all cynical about the modern world?
Lenny's voice (*as Myrtle; over the speaker*) Well it's absolutely pouring with rain here actually.

Lenny is appalled. Letitia isn't asking the planned questions

Letitia Myrtle, what can you tell us about your new book?
Lenny's voice (*as Myrtle; over the speaker*) Well it's absolutely pouring with rain here actually.
Gus (*into the microphone*) Oh bloody hell.
Lenny (*stepping into the breach*) So, Myrtle, dear — how is the weather over there at the moment?
Lenny's voice (*as Myrtle; over the speaker*) The book is packed with sex and intrigue on every page.
Letitia I see. So, Myrtle you're not bothered with political correctness then?

Gus and Dee Dee are baffled. The question is not on the cards

Lenny (*checking the questions*) Did you hear that, Myrtle?
Letitia Myrtle, Myrtle?
Lenny's voice (*as Myrtle; over the speaker; after a pause*) Well it's absolutely pouring with rain here actually.
Lenny It's probably a bad line. Hallo. Myrtle. (*Checking the list of questions*) Perhaps you could tell us what you make of the political situation in the UK? Tony Blair, Gordon Brown?
Lenny's voice (*as Myrtle; over the speaker*) Irritable bowel syndrome from time to time.
Dee Dee Grampi, give it here ... (*Into the microphone*) Question thirteen, Dad ...
Lenny (*checking the list*) Right ... Er ... Myrtle ... Letitia wants to know what you think women today are really looking for?
Lenny's voice (*as Myrtle; over the speaker*) A nice plate of jellied eels.
Letitia Absolutely. So Myrtle, what is it makes you so prolific?
Lenny's voice (*as Myrtle; over the speaker*) Lots of roughage and plenty of fresh fruit.

Letitia takes the notes and tears them up

Letitia To hell with these. I believe in flying by the seat of my pants, don't you, Myrtle?
Lenny's voice (*as Myrtle; over the speaker*) Oh yes, I've always enjoyed highland dancing.
Lenny Myrtle, Myrtle, have you been at the tequilla?

Dee Dee repeatedly hits two keys on the machine, alternating between them

Lenny's voice (*as Myrtle; over the speaker*) Yes. No. Yes. No. God Save The Queen.

There is a knock on the basement front door. Lenny opens the door

Fran enters

Letitia A visitor, viewers. I'm just going to go with the flow.
Lenny (*to Fran*) Hallo.
Fran Hallo.
Letitia Hallo. Hallo, Fran. Welcome. We're on air.
Lenny "Mind Your Own Business".
Fran I am so sorry.
Letitia (*to the camera*) What a bonus, viewers. This is Fran, Lenny's ex. How lovely to see you. We are just having a chat, a conference call with Myrtle. She's in Brazil.
Lenny (*worried*) Way up the Amazon.
Fran (*getting the picture*) Oh, I see ...
Letitia Myrtle, do you hear that, Fran has arrived. Isn't that grand?

Gus drops his head on the table in despair. He presses a button

Lenny's voice (*as Myrtle; over the speaker*) No thank you, I'm going to bed.
Fran Hallo there, Myrtle. How are you doing?
Lenny's voice (*as Myrtle; over the speaker*) I rode an elephant once in Bangalore.
Fran Oh good. I've never done that. Have you. Lenny?
Gus (*into the microphone*) For God's sake, Lenny, she's going to let the cat out of the bag.
Lenny No ... Er ... No ... Nor have I ever let a cat out of a bag.
Fran (*meaning it*) Me neither. Never.
Gus (*into the microphone*) Ask her what the hell is she doing here?

Act II   59

Lenny What the hell is you doing here? What are you doing here? Weren't you going to ——?
Gus (*into the microphone*)Barbados.
Lenny — Barbados — to marry —
Gus (*into the microphone*) Luigi.
Lenny — Luigi.
Fran Well done.
Lenny You miss your flight?
Fran No.
Lenny Flight delayed?
Fran Cancelled. The whole damn thing cancelled.
Lenny The lime green dress — the beach ...
Fran The calypso band — the full moon. All cancelled.
Letitia Oh I am so sorry, Fran.
Lenny You can't cancel the full moon.
Letitia (*hearing Ron on her earpiece*) No, no, no, Ron ... (*She advances to address the camera*) Don't cut, for God's sake. You great stupid prat. Take two ... Action. (*She quickly gets back into position and character*) Oh, I am so sorry, Fran. So you're not marrying Luigi? What happened?
Fran I dumped him.
Letitia You dumped him?
Dee Dee (*to Gus*) She dumped him?
Gus (*into the microphone*)She dumped him?
Lenny You dumped him?
Lenny's voice (*as Myrtle; over the speaker*) You dumped him?

The next two lines are optional in the event of Myrtle's line not being properly heard. (It's a tough cue for the sound dept with the audience reaction)

All I beg your pardon?
Lenny's voice (*as Myrtle; over the speaker*) You dumped him?
Fran Yup. I dumped him.
Letitia What do you think of that, Myrtle?
Lenny's voice (*as Myrtle; over the speaker*) I had my tonsils out when I was nine.
Letitia I beg your pardon?
Lenny's voice (*as Myrtle; over the speaker*) There's sex and intrigue on every page.
Lenny Shut up. Shut up.

Gus is at a loss which key to press

Lenny's voice (*as Myrtle; over the speaker*) I'm a Taurus with Virgo rising.

Letitia So tell me, Fran, what happened with Luigi?
Fran When I arrived at the check-in there he was in his Armani bomber jacket and his white moccasins and his Tommy Hilfiger aftershave and I said to myself, is this what I really want in life?
Lenny And how did you answer?
Fran Well, you know sometimes when you're in a restaurant and you order, say, the *boeuf bourginogne* and then when it comes you suddenly realize that all you want is just an omelette.
Lenny An omelette?
Lenny What kind of omelette?
Fran Just a plain omelette.
Lenny You mean with just eggs?
Fran Well yes — with just eggs.
Letitia So you sent it back, did you? The *boeuf bourginogne*.
Fran Yup.
Letitia How did Luigi take it?
Fran Not at all well.
Letitia "Dump not lest ye be dumped," I say. I remember the first time it happened to me. The rat.
Fran To you? You were dumped? How did you cope?
Letitia I went straight round to his house and slashed his tyres.
Fran A futile gesture.
Letitia It certainly was. I got the wrong car.
Gus (*into the microphone*) What's *boeuf bourginogne*?
Lenny (*on a reflex*) Stew.

Fran and Letitia, in unison, turn to Lenny in surprise; what's she talking about?

Lenny Let him stew.
Letitia But Fran, I don't understand *why*. It wasn't just the white moccasins, was it?
Fran No, actually, it was something Myrtle said the other evening.
Letitia What was that?
Fran She said bastards are all very well in the short term but if they don't know your dress size or remember your birthday, what's the point? (*To Lenny*) There's nothing at all wrong with the kind of man who brings you the odd cup of Horlicks.
Letitia Exactly. It's easy to spice up a dull man but you can never housetrain a bastard.
Lenny Myrtle, you must have had enough of this?
Lenny's voice (*as Myrtle; over the speaker*) No, no.
Lenny You must be tired.
Lenny's voice (*as Myrtle; over the speaker*) No no.
Fran Can we talk some more?

Act II

Lenny's voice (*as Myrtle; over the speaker*) Yes, yes.
Fran (*looking at Lenny wickedly*) You don't think Lenny will mind?
Lenny's voice (*as Myrtle; over the speaker*) Who cares ...
Fran (*playing him at his own game*) What do you think of him?

Gus presses the key with relish

Lenny's voice (*as Myrtle; over the speaker*) Pretty wet actually and full of dry rot.
Fran (*in control*) Do you remember? We were talking about your book, Myrtle? The last scene, do you remember?
Lenny's voice (*as Myrtle; over the speaker*) Yes, yes.
Fran In the cave. Up the mountain.
Lenny's voice (*as Myrtle; over the speaker*) Yes, yes.
Fran There's a terrific storm. They're sharing a picnic.
Lenny's voice (*as Myrtle; over the speaker*) Yes, yes.
Fran And we talked about a re-write for Joshua. You were going to have him tell Ingrid all the things he missed about her, the details of how and why he's still in love with her, remember?
Lenny's voice (*as Myrtle; over the speaker*) Yes. Yes.
Lenny No. No.
Letitia What kind of things, Myrtle?
Fran Things that could melt a girl's heart; it was such a beautiful speech — quite irresistible. And I realized it was the kind of thing that I was never going to hear from him.
Lenny The *boeuf bourginogne.*
Fran Yeah. Not in a million years.
Letitia (*to the camera*) What was it, the speech, Myrtle? How did it go?
Fran You must remember.
Lenny (*frantically*) No. You don't do you?
Lenny's voice (*as Myrtle; over the speaker*) Yes, I do.
Lenny It's none of your business, Auntie.
Letitia What do you say to that, Myrtle?
Lenny's voice (*as Myrtle; over the speaker*) It's absolutely pouring with rain here actually.
Gus (*into the microphone*) Tell her, Lenny. Tell her once and for all. Tell her loud and clear.
Dee Dee Go on, Dad. Go for it. It's now or never.
Lenny (*dithering, then with resolve*) Right. Are we still on air? Is the camera running?
Letitia Yes. I lost the will to live five minutes ago.
Lenny (*to the camera*) Hallo, viewers. All of you out there. Here is an announcement. This is Fran, the woman I ——
Letitia What are you doing?

Fran Have you got something to say? To me? Publicly?

Lenny nods

Letitia Oh viewers, suddenly I'm getting rosy pink.
Fran Well? On you go.

Lenny freezes

Gus (*into the microphone*) Get on with it ... (*Prompting*) It's about ...
Lenny It's about ...
Gus (*into the microphone*) Me.
Lenny (*confused*) You?
Gus (*into the microphone*) And her.
Lenny You and her?
Fran Me?
Lenny Yes — me and me. You. And how — and how I ...

Letitia goes DS *and addresses the camera*

Letitia (*furiously*) No, Ron, you great steaming pillock, leave the camera running. This is reality TV for God's sake. Reality TV with *real* reality. Action.
Lenny No. Wait. Right. (*To Fran*) Sit down, Fran.

Fran sits

Eat those ...

Lenny takes the Liquorice Allsorts from the desk and hands them to Fran, then strips off his jacket

Right. OK ... Right. Here we go ... Action! (*To Ron and Fran*) This is about ... How and why and for how long I've ... I've ...
Gus (*into the microphone*) Loved you.
Lenny (*nodding*) Yes. (*He realizes he has to say it*) Loved you. I never stopped — not for a moment. Never could.
All Go on.
Fran Go on.
Lenny's voice (*as Myrtle; over the speaker*) Give her the details, you great daft prune.
Lenny I love the b-bl-blueness of y-yo-our eyes ——

A full orchestral backing fades up under Lenny's singing of the following

Act II 63

(*Singing to the tune of "Men of Harlech"*) and the sound of your laughter, and the smoothness of your skin ... *I love you.*

They kiss

CURTAIN

FURNITURE AND PROPERTY LIST

ACT I

On stage: LIVING-ROOM
                Sofa
                Chair
                Cupboard. *In it:* wig block with wig, full garish make-up, jewellery
                Desk. *On it:* laptop computer, intercom. *In drawer:* **Lenny**'s wallet containing ten pound note
                Small video camera on tripod with microphone
                On shelf: bottle of wine and glasses

                STUDY
                Integral fish tank
                Chairs
                Desk. *On it:* laptop computer, intercom, normal telephone, framed photograph. *In drawer:* pink mobile phone, letter, tiny loudspeaker
                On shelf: chart
                Broom handle

Off stage: Fat cigar, cue cards (**Gus**)
                Cue cards (**Lenny**)

Personal: **Gus**: coins
                Dee Dee: box containing tiny earpiece
                Fran: handbag containing Liquorice Allsorts

ACT II

Set: LIVING-ROOM
                Candles
                Tray. *On it:* plates, dishes, empty wine glasses
                Wine bottle
                Bag containing Arsenal babygro

                STUDY
                Loudspeaker (live)

Furniture and Property List

Off stage: Bags of shopping (**Dee Dee** and **Fran**)

Personal: **Lenny**: handbag containing battered copy of the pink mobile phone
Dee Dee: handbag containing photograph
Fran: *in handbag*: manuscript, mobile phone

LIGHTING PLOT

Practical fittings: lights in fish tank
Composite set: two interiors. The same throughout

ACT I

To open: General interior lighting on living-room and study; fish tank lights on

No cues

ACT II

To open:	General interior lighting on living-room only	
Cue 1	**Gus** exits *Bring up lights in study and fish tank*	(Page 42)
Cue 2	**Lenny** exits up the stairs *Fade living-room lights to black-out*	(Page 43)
Cue 3	**Lenny** drops the mobile into the fish tank *Flicker fish tank and living-room lights*	(Page 47)
Cue 4	**Fran** exits to the street *Fade study lights and fish tank lights*	(Page 48)
Cue 5	**Lenny** exits to the kitchen *Bring up lights on living-room*	(Page 48)
Cue 6	**Gus** hangs up *Bring up lights on study*	(Page 50)

EFFECTS PLOT

ACT I

Cue 1	**Gus**: "… is due out this Christmas." *Telephone rings*	(Page 2)
Cue 2	**Gus**: "Could be fun." *Mobile phone rings in the study*	(Page 2)
Cue 3	**Lenny**: "… seafood risotto, I expect." *Upper front doorbell rings*	(Page 13)
Cue 4	**Gus**: "Hallo. Yes." *Activate offstage microphone for* **Fran**	(Page 13)
Cue 5	**Lenny** exits into the kitchen *Upper front doorbell rings*	(Page 24)
Cue 6	**Gus** dials the phone *Mobile phone rings*	(Page 27)
Cue 7	**Lenny** presses a button on the laptop *Ferocious ocean storm from laptop*	(Page 27)
Cue 8	**Lenny** turns up the sea sound effects *Increase volume of ocean storm effect*	(Page 28)
Cue 9	**Lenny** presses another key *Farmyard noises and a long "Moooo" from laptop*	(Page 28)
Cue 10	**Lenny** presses another key *Rain forest sound effects from laptop*	(Page 28)
Cue 11	**Lenny**: "… at the moment, Letitia." *Loud laughing sound of a monkey from laptop*	(Page 28)
Cue 12	**Fran**: "Are you all right?" *Monkey laughs again*	(Page 31)

ACT II

Cue 13	**Fran:** "He needs to get that quite clear." *Mobile phone rings*	(Page 47)
Cue 14	**Lenny** slams the bag on the desk *Ringing stops then resumes in a damaged tone*	(Page 47)
Cue 15	**Lenny** hits the bag several times with his shoe *Ring-tone changes to injured sound, then signals a painful death; then there is the sound of a hospital heart monitor "flatlining"*	(Page 47)
Cue 16	**Fran** hits the redial button *Feeble ringing tone*	(Page 47)
Cue 17	**Lenny** drops the mobile into the fishtank *Water in fishtank bubbles frantically*	(Page 47)
Cue 18	**Dee Dee** presses a key on the laptop **Lenny**'s *voice from laptop; dialogue as p. 49*	(Page 49)
Cue 19	**Dee Dee:** "Is **Letitia** a stupid old cow?" **Lenny**'s *voice from laptop; dialogue as p. 49*	(Page 49)
Cue 20	**Gus:** " ... eleven million people." **Lenny**'s *voice from laptop; dialogue as p. 49*	(Page 49)
Cue 21	**Lenny** (*voice-over*) " ... a piece of cake." *Landline telephone rings*	(Page 49)
Cue 22	**Gus** presses a key on the laptop *Landline telephone rings*	(Page 51)
Cue 23	**Gus** presses a key on the laptop **Lenny**'s *voice from loudspeaker; dialogue as p. 52*	(Page 52)
Cue 24	**Gus** presses another key on the laptop **Lenny**'s *voice from loudspeaker; dialogue as p. 52*	(Page 52)
Cue 25	**Dee Dee:** "Here we go, Grampi." *Telephone rings in study*	(Page 55)
Cue 26	**Gus** presses a key on the laptop **Lenny**'s *voice from loudspeaker; dialogue as p. 55*	(Page 55)

Effects Plot

Cue 27	**Lenny**: " ... 'Mind Your Own Business'." **Lenny**'s *voice from loudspeaker; dialogue as p. 55*	(Page 55)
Cue 28	**Gus**: "Hold on ... " He presses a key *Voice of* **Sexy-Voiced Woman**, *dialogue as p.55*	(Page 55)
Cue 29	**Gus** turns the radio connection off *Cut radio sound*	(Page 56)
Cue 30	**Lenny**: "Auntie, can we just ask you a few questions?" **Lenny**'s *voice from loudspeaker; dialogue as p. 56*	(Page 56)
Cue 31	**Gus** flounders with the computer **Lenny**'s *voice from loudspeaker; dialogue as p. 56*	(Page 56)
Cue 32	**Gus** finds the right key and presses it **Lenny**'s *voice from loudspeaker; dialogue as p. 56*	(Page 56)
Cue 33	**Lenny**: "I love you, Auntie." **Lenny**'s *voice from loudspeaker; dialogue as p. 56*	(Page 56)
Cue 34	**Gus**: "Help ..." He presses a key very firmly **Lenny**'s *voice from loudspeaker; dialogue as p. 56*	(Page 56)
Cue 35	**Gus** presses a key uncertainly **Lenny**'s *voice from loudspeaker; dialogue as p. 57*	(Page 57)
Cue 36	**Letitia**: " ... the modern world?" **Lenny**'s *voice from loudspeaker; dialogue as p. 57*	(Page 57)
Cue 37	**Letitia**: " ... about your new book?" **Lenny**'s *voice from loudspeaker; dialogue as p. 57*	(Page 57)
Cue 38	**Lenny**: " ... at the moment?" **Lenny**'s *voice from loudspeaker; dialogue as p. 57*	(Page 57)
Cue 39	**Letitia**: " ... Myrtle, Myrtle?" **Lenny**'s *voice from loudspeaker; dialogue as p. 57*	(Page 57)
Cue 40	**Lenny**: "Tony Blair, Gordon Brown?" **Lenny**'s *voice from loudspeaker; dialogue as p. 57*	(Page 57)
Cue 41	**Lenny**: " ... really looking for?" **Lenny**'s *voice from loudspeaker; dialogue as p. 57*	(Page 57)
Cue 42	**Letitia**: "... makes you so prolific?" **Lenny**'s *voice from loudspeaker; dialogue as p. 57*	(Page 57)

Cue 43	Letitia: " ... don't you, Myrtle?" Lenny's voice from loudspeaker; dialogue as p. 58	(Page 58)
Cue 44	Dee Dee repeatedly hits two keys, alternating between them Lenny's voice from loudspeaker; dialogue as p. 58	(Page 58)
Cue 45	Gus presses a key Lenny's voice from loudspeaker; dialogue as p. 58	(Page 58)
Cue 46	Fran: "How are you doing?" Lenny's voice from loudspeaker; dialogue as p. 58	(Page 58)
Cue 47	Lenny: "You dumped him?" Lenny's voice from loudspeaker; dialogue as p. 59	(Page 59)
Cue 48	All: "I beg your pardon?" Lenny's voice from loudspeaker; dialogue as p. 59	(Page 59)
Cue 49	Letitia: "What do you think of that, Myrtle?" Lenny's voice from loudspeaker; dialogue as p. 59	(Page 59)
Cue 50	Letitia: "I beg your pardon?" Lenny's voice from loudspeaker; dialogue as p. 59	(Page 59)
Cue 51	Lenny: "Shut up. Shut up." Gus presses a key Lenny's voice from loudspeaker; dialogue as p. 59	(Page 59)
Cue 52	Lenny: " ... had enough of this?" Lenny's voice from loudspeaker; dialogue as p. 60	(Page 60)
Cue 53	Lenny: "You must be tired." Lenny's voice from loudspeaker; dialogue as p. 60	(Page 60)
Cue 54	Fran: "Can we talk some more?" Lenny's voice from loudspeaker; dialogue as p. 61	(Page 60)
Cue 55	Fran: "You don't think Lenny will mind?" Lenny's voice from loudspeaker; dialogue as p. 61	(Page 61)
Cue 56	Gus presses the key with relish Lenny's voice from loudspeaker; dialogue as p. 61	(Page 61)
Cue 57	Fran: "The last scene, do you remember?" Lenny's voice from loudspeaker; dialogue as p. 61	(Page 61)

Effects Plot

Cue 58	**Fran**: "Up the mountain." **Lenny**'s *voice from loudspeaker; dialogue as p. 61*	(Page 61)
Cue 59	**Fran**: "They're sharing a picnic." **Lenny**'s *voice from loudspeaker; dialogue as p. 61*	(Page 61)
Cue 60	**Fran**: " ... still in love with her, remember?" **Lenny**'s *voice from loudspeaker; dialogue as p. 61*	(Page 61)
Cue 61	**Lenny**: "No. You don't, do you?" **Lenny**'s *voice from loudspeaker; dialogue as p. 62*	(Page 61)
Cue 62	**Letitia**: "What do you say to that, Myrtle?" **Lenny**'s *voice from loudspeaker; dialogue as p. 61*	(Page 61)
Cue 63	**Fran**: "Go on." **Lenny**'s *voice from loudspeaker; dialogue as p. 62*	(Page 62)
Cue 64	**Lenny**: "I love the b-bl-blueness of y-yo-our eyes ———" *Fade up full orchestral backing: "Men of Harlech"*	(Page 62)

A licence issued by Samuel French Ltd to perform this play does not include permission to use the Incidental music specified in this copy. Where the place of performance is already licensed by the PERFORMING RIGHT SOCIETY a return of the music used must be made to them. If the place of performance is not so licensed then application should be made to the PERFORMING RIGHT SOCIETY, 29-33 Berners Street, London W1T 4AB.

A separate and additional licence from PHONOGRAPHIC PERFORMANCES LTD, 1 Upper James Street, London W1R 3HG is needed whenever commercial recordings are used.

www.ingramcontent.com/pod-product-compliance
Ingram Content Group UK Ltd.
Pitfield, Milton Keynes, MK11 3LW, UK
UKHW030419280625
460178UK00007B/243